AMERICAN FASHION TRAVEL

Designers on the Go

© Council of Fashion Designers of America
© 2011 Assouline Publishing
601 West 26th Street, 18th Floor
New York, NY 10001 USA
Tel.: 212 989-6810 Fax: 212 647-0005
www.assouline.com
Color separation by Luc Alexis Chasleries
Printed in China
ISBN: 978 2 7594 0509 1

COUNCIL OF FASHION DESIGNERS OF AMERICA

Foreword by Diane von Furstenberg

AMERICAN FASHION TRAVEL
Designers on the Go

ASSOULINE

The very welcoming people of the Republic of Vanuatu

Foreword by Diane von Furstenberg

Life is a journey, and every trip is an adventure.

Ten years ago, Christian Louboutin and I decided to go to Uzbekistan and follow the Silk Road. Neither of us knew much about Uzbekistan, but it sounded like it could be an adventure, and we loved the lore of the Silk Road. We arrived in Tashkent, the capital, not really knowing anything about how to go about traveling through the country. I usually try to have at least one contact in each of the places I go, and I had the name of a woman there, Zulfia. Luckily, her son had a car, and we drove all around Uzbekistan with him—to Samarkand, Bukhara, and Khiva. It was like being on a frontier. We slept one night in an old Koranic school, another night in somebody's house. That was a great trip.

For me, traveling is a regular thing, but always a privilege and an extraordinary experience. You go somewhere and you don't know what's going to happen or what you'll see. I love the feeling of expectation and potential discovery. I am a great traveler, because I love to travel alone and am not afraid. I love to discover new things. I believe that bad trips are rare. If there is an accident or if something goes wrong, of course that changes the tone of the trip—but otherwise, every trip is a good one.

I travel a lot. I'm not necessarily on a plane every week, but if you were to look at my diaries, you would see that I go around the world many times every year. I move around a lot. I like to say that I am a jet-setter only because I really do take a lot of jets.

I will always remember one of my first trips: I was nine years old and living in Belgium. My parents put me on a train alone to Paris. I felt so grown-up and it was so exhilarating. Every time I travel today, I feel that same exhilaration.

I love the unknown, the unexpected encounter, and that is why I relish traveling by myself. I like meeting new people and seeing things I've never before witnessed. I wonder about people who travel with an entourage—what's the point?

Even before I had ever traveled, I saw the world through books. Reading is another way to travel, to discover. Within a book's pages lies the opportunity to take a trip, one that can be further informed by maps. When I was young, I read the comic strip *The Adventures of Tintin*, and was so inspired by the young Belgian reporter who had adventures all around the world. Through reading about what Tintin did, I discovered geography. Today, when I am about to embark on an adventure, I always channel him.

For fashion designers, travel is necessary—we probably travel more than people in other industries. Certainly there's the essential travel for work—to fabric shows, mills, factories, and such—but travel, whether to museums, markets, or monuments, also serves as a major source of inspiration. Conversely, fashion is also very much a part of traveling.

For me, traveling and living are the same. How you travel is a symbol of your life, and I think it's very important to travel light. I pack for every three days or so, and that is my key to flying around as much as I do. Packing is an art, and one that I have grown very adept at over the years. No matter how lightly I pack, it's still too much. These days, if I have a camera, my iPad, and hiking boots, I feel I'm prepared for anything. To know how to pack is to know how to live. Life is a journey: people come in, people leave, you see new things, and you move on.

My husband and I have a boat. It goes around the world, and I go where it goes. Wherever we moor, we hike and discover, venturing into jungles and unfamiliar environments. Then at night, we go back to our boat.

One of the best places we visited by boat in the last year is Vanuatu, an island nation in the South Pacific. I also love to travel to Asia and South America. I haven't been to Patagonia and I haven't been to Mongolia—those are two places that I'd like to go.

With every trip comes the unexpected, and that becomes part of your experience when you travel. You have to be very open and spontaneous and ready to change your plans. When you meet someone or see something, be prepared to go there. It's a wonderful mode to operate in. Travel is truly so much a part of who I am.

We hope travel is a part of who you are as well, and that seeing the special places featured here inspires you to pack your bags and visit one of them. Create an adventure of your own!

Diane von Furstenberg

President | Council of Fashion Designers of America

On the volcanoes of the Aeolian Islands, in Southern Italy

Table of Contents

50	Adam Lippes	120	Deborah Lloyd	121	Karen Erickson
15	Adrienne Landau	109	Dennis Basso	97	Kay Unger
13	Alexander Wang	28	Diane von Furstenberg	22	Keanan Duffty
66	Amy Chan	106	Donna Karan	70	Keren Craig
15	Amy Smilovic	84	Douglas Hannant	24	Kevin Carrigan
34	Andrew Buckler	99	Edward Wilkerson	41	Lana Marks
65	Andrew Fezza	37	Elie Tahari	63	Lela Rose
26	Behnaz Sarafpour	112	Erica Courtney	75	Lisa Mayock
38	Betsey Johnson	118	Fiona Kotur Marin	68	Lubov Azria
96	Bibhu Mohapatra	91	Francisco Costa	58	Marcella Lindeberg
59	Billy Reid	72	Georgina Chapman	111	Marcia Sherrill
42	Blake Kuwahara	52	Gilles Mendel	69	Max Azria
82	Carole Hochman	89	Henry Jacobson	88	Michel Kramer-Metraux
35	Carolina Amato	90	Isaac Manevitz	60	Mimi So
85	Catherine Malandrino	47	Italo Zucchelli	14	Mish Tworkowski
30	Cheryl Finnegan	65	Jackie Rogers	80	Monica Rich Kosann
80	Chris Benz	21	Jeffrey Costello &	77	Monique Péan
113	Christian Roth		Robert Tagliapietra	67	Naeem Khan
54	Christina &	16	Jeffrey Banks	17	Nanette Lepore
	Swaim Hutson	61	John Bartlett	56	Narciso Rodriguez
86	Colette Malouf	57	John Patrick	16	Nicole Miller
115	Cynthia Rowley	94	Josie Natori	66	Norma Kamali
104	David Meister	110	Julie Chaiken	92	Pamella Roland

14	Paul Morelli	31	Sam Shipley & Jeff Halmos	10	Tommy Hilfiger
27	Peter Som	36	Sang A Im-Propp	32	Tory Burch
40	Phillip Lim	95	Selima Salaun	46	Trina Turk
48	R. Scott French	51	Shane Baum	41	Ulrich Grimm
108	Rachel Roy	12	Simon Alcantara	102	Vanessa Noel
100	Rafe Totengco	64	Simon Spurr	98	Vera Wang
20	Rebecca Minkoff	74	Sophie Buhai	44	Waris Ahluwalia
62	Ricky Serbin	81	Stephen Dweck	31	Yeohlee Teng
61	Robert Danes	119	Sue Stemp	25	Yigal Azrouël
78	Robert Geller	116	Sully Bonnelly		
76	Robert Rodriguez	67	Sylvia Heisel		
13	Robert Stock	18	Tina Lutz		
114	Ron Chereskin				

123	Travel Questionnaires
138	Fashionable Address Book
142	CFDA Member List
144	Acknowledgments

Charles Bridge, Prague

Tommy Hilfiger

Whenever I can I travel to.

PARIS !

Plane, train, boat, motorcycle, or car?

Plane, of course !

My fondest travel memory.

my Longest Vacation

The restaurant I would go farthest for.

Bukhara
New Delhi, India

My favorite city.

New York
London

My favorite market.

Turkish
Bazaar
Istanbul

Simon Alcantara

My favorite destination.
Adrère Amellal Ecolodge
in the Siwa Oasis, Egypt.

Alexander Wang

My favorite destination. *Rio de Janeiro*

The best hotel or place to stay.
George V in Paris, or Conrad in Tokyo.

I'm always searching for the perfect. *Spa.*

On the beach
in Rio de Janeiro, Brazil

Robert Stock, *ROBERT GRAHAM*

My fondest travel memory.
I had been working for two days with Ralph Lauren when I was informed that I had to travel to Italy. That in itself was a shock because I had never been out of the country. Then I was informed that I was to leave in two days. There was no time to prepare—just go! It was exciting and filled with many firsts.

My favorite store.
Hidetaka Fukaya. He's the only Japanese cobbler in the whole city of Florence. He makes everything by hand. The level of quality and precision in each pair of his shoes is unparalleled. They're stunning.

Always in my carry-on luggage.
Burt's Bees hand sanitizer—there's never enough.

Mish Tworkowski, *MISH NEW YORK*

The best hotel or place to stay. 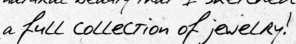 The Wakaya Club & Spa, in Fiji!!
It is the most intensely wonderful island in the most beautiful place on earth. My partner, Joseph, and I went there for a rest, but from the second I arrived I felt so inspired by the natural beauty that I sketched a full collection of jewelry!

Joseph and me on a camel ride in Egypt

Our welcome sign at Wakaya with some shells I collected

Paul Morelli

My favorite beach. Long Beach Island, New Jersey

Whenever I can I travel to. Europe

My favorite store. Carversville General Store, Carversville, PA.

Adrienne Landau

Camping in the canyons of Sedona, Arizona, with my vintage Mustang

My favorite guide or travel writing.

My Hungarian grandfather's stories about traveling the world. He always had so much fun!

I'm always searching for the perfect.

Man or cookies.

My preferred luggage. *Vintage Louis Vuitton.*

Peace, culture, or adventure.

I am always up for a crazy adventure. It's the gypsy in me.

Amy Smilovic, *TIBI*

My fondest travel memory.

Visiting Prague this summer with my family and watching my husband show our two boys where he was born and how his family escaped the country in 1968.

My favorite beach. *Sea Island, GA*

The best snow. *Bachelor Gulch, CO*

A place I will never go. *Mall of America, in Bloomington, MN.*

Charles Bridge, Prague

Jeffrey Banks

A view of the lake near Goshen, CT

My favorite guide or travel writing.

Time Out's foreign editions are remarkably good.

My preferred luggage. *My Ralph Lauren tartan luggage.*

Jet lag remedy. *A quick hot chocolate and then shopping. Guaranteed to work every time.*

Nicole Miller

Whenever I can I travel to. *San Miguel de Allende, Mexico*

My favorite guide or travel writing. *Where to Wear shopping guides.*

My favorite store. *Oak on Bond St., NYC.*

My favorite market. *Sag Harbor Farmers' Market, in the Hamptons, NY.*

Jet lag remedy. *Double espresso!*

Always in my suitcase. *Exercise clothes.*

My preferred luggage. *Swiss Army.*

Nanette Lepore

My fondest travel memory. *My parents waking my siblings and me during a drive through New Mexico, so that we could all watch the sun rise over a desert mesa.*

The restaurant I would go farthest for. *Da Adolfo in Positano, Italy. It can only be reached by boat, and I love it for the sexy sailors, the sandy floor, and the delicious pasta con sarde.*

Always in my carry-on luggage. *A bikini and a cocktail dress.*

The fish at Da Adolfo

One of my go-to bikinis

Childhood memory: Jeannie, James, Michelle, and me in the desert

Tina Lutz, *LUTZ & PATMOS*

My favorite destination/ Whenever I can I travel to/ The best hotel or place to stay.

I grew up with parents who are passionate world travelers. Their mantra was, and still is, that the world is too big to go to the same place twice. As beautiful as a place was, we would never go back.

I broke with this family tradition after discovering the Rockhouse Hotel in Jamaica in 1993.

My wedding at the Rockhouse in Jamaica

Once I saw the fourteen thatched-roof huts set on the cliffs of the westernmost tip of Jamaica, I fell in love with the place. It's the best spot for sunsets. The huts were in rough condition but magical, nestled among eight acres of lush gardens. Shortly after, and by complete coincidence, my friend Paul bought the Rockhouse, and my love story with the place got started. The first

My favorite travel
guide websites are:

blacktomato.co.uk

mrandmrssmith.com

tablehotels.com

superfuture.com/supertravel

year, it was closed for renovations, and I ended up going six times as part of the design crew. A restaurant was suspended directly over the water, a horizon pool was built into the rocks, a reception area was constructed, and more rooms were added. Slowly I saw the Rockhouse grow to be what it is now: a beautiful eco-boutique hotel with a spa and two award-winning restaurants. It's my home away from home.

My husband, Justin, also fell in love with the Rockhouse, and so there was no question that we wanted to get married there. With Paul's help, we took the hotel over for one week in 2002 and had friends and family fly in from all over the world. The dress code was in the spirit of the casual feeling of the place—no suits, no gowns—and everybody dressed in white.

Now our son, Lou, is counting the days until we go back for New Year's. It's become our own family tradition to return year after year, and for all of our other travels, we follow my parents' mantra and never go back to the same place twice.

Rebecca Minkoff

My fondest travel memory.

During the summer of 2010, I traveled by a gullet to **Turkey.** *It was so beautiful and peaceful to be disconnected from the world like that.*

Jet lag remedy. *A facial with skin guru Joanna Vargas.*

A neighboring sailboat

My new favorite book—highly recommend it

66 Photographs are the perfect souvenir! 99

Gavin and me taking advantage of our last day sunbathing

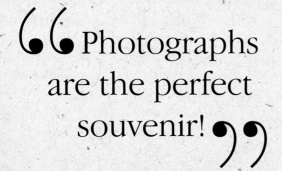

A genuine Turkish breakfast—O is for olives

Traditional olive oil soaps

Jeffrey Costello & Robert Tagliapietra,

COSTELLO TAGLIAPIETRA

My favorite destination. *New England*

Whenever we can we travel to. *Maine or Provincetown, MA.*

Our favorite store. *Fortnum & Mason in London.*

En route, we wear. *Suspenders and comfortable pants.*

Always in our suitcase. *Lots of plaid; dog treats if Sam, our dog, is with us; our beard brush and laptop; Canson sketchbooks; an ipod; and a bunch of books.*

Always in our carry-on luggage. *Same as above—we never check our bags—the benefit of sharing a wardrobe for sixteen years!*

Night view in New England

Us on Race Point Beach, in Provincetown, MA

Keanan Duffty, *SLINKY VAGABOND INC*

My favorite destination. **Goa, India**

My fondest travel memory. New York, for the first time in 1989.

Whenever I can I travel to. The farthest place I can get to.

The best snow. Not into Snow. It's too Cold. ☺

My favorite city. Shanghai

The best museum. Victoria + Albert museum, London.

Jet lag remedy. Homeopathic Jet Lag Pills.

Peace, culture, or adventure. Always a Combination of Peace Culture + adventure.

An ideal trip would be. To a brand new place.

A place I will never go. There is nowhere I would not visit.

The perfect souvenir. Something hand made.

En route, I wear. Some Slip-on Sneakers.

Always in my carry-on luggage. Really Good Music.

The best hotel or place to stay. Hotel Condesa, Mexico City.

My favorite store. James Smith & Sons Umbrellas, London.

The restaurant I would go farthest for. Ristorante Zaira, Siena, Tuscany.

My preferred airline. Virgin, for fun, first class.

Kevin Carrigan, *ck CALVIN KLEIN, CALVIN KLEIN & CALVIN KLEIN JEANS*

My favorite destination. My house in Bellport, Long Island.

My fondest travel memory. Angkor Wat, Cambodia, for my fortieth birthday.

Whenever I can I travel to. Como Shambhala and Ubud, both in Bali, Indonesia.

My favorite guide or travel writing. Bruce Chatwin.

My favorite beach. Bondi Beach, Australia

The best snow. Pontresina, Switzerland

My favorite city. Rio de Janeiro, Brazil

The best museum. Tate Modern, in London.

The best hotel or place to stay. Como Shambhala Estate, in Bali.

The world's best shopping street. Omotesando, Tokyo

My favorite store. 10 Corso Como, in Milan, Italy.

My favorite market. Les Puces at Porte de Clignancourt, Paris.

The restaurant I would go farthest for. Icebergs, Bondi Beach, Australia.

My preferred airline. Singapore Airlines.

My preferred luggage. A carry-on, whenever possible.

Jet lag remedy. Sleep aids and a good workout.

Always in my suitcase. Too many shoes.

Always in my carry-on luggage. Jurlique skin care.

Yigal Azrouël

Sunset in Playa Negra, Costa Rica

"I'm always searching for the perfect wave."

Me in Playa Negra, Costa Rica

My favorite destination.

Playa Negra, Costa Rica

Whenever I can I travel to.
Costa Rica. I have not discovered a place that I love as much. I love to surf and when I get time to travel, I try to go.

Plane, train, boat, motorcycle, or car?
Motorcycle, for leisurely drives.

En route, I wear.
Sweatpants, flip flops, and a T-shirt. I like to travel in comfort.

Behnaz Sarafpour

A street market
in Mumbai, India

At a camel farm outside Riyadh,
Saudi Arabia

At the Taj Lake Palace
in Udaipur, India

Female construction workers at the
Monsoon Palace in Udaipur, India

One of the local men with his
camel in Jaipur, India

Peter Som

The harvest moon, as seen from a friend's house in Wainscott, NY

My favorite destination. Anywhere with a beach!

My fondest travel memory. Our family took trips every summer, starting when I was very young. Most of my best memories involve my sister and me making fools of ourselves, and my parents wondering what went wrong.

Always in my suitcase. Only what I need—I am a light packer!

Always in my carry-on luggage.
— Bose noise-reduction headphones
— Clark's Botanicals lip balm
— Moleskine sketch pad
— Leica D-Lux 3
— Kashi TLC Chewy Granola Bars

An ideal trip would be.
Safari in Kenya; dinner in Paris; spa in Therme Vals, Switzerland; and beach in St. Bart's—no planes involved! How do we make this happen?

A place I will never go. Never say never, but I'd probably avoid any war-torn countries.

In St. Bart's, en route to Gustavia

66 I'm not big on souvenirs, except for food souvenirs. 99

27

Diane von Furstenberg

My favorite destination. *Wherever our boat goes.*

My fondest travel memory. *Usually the LAST one.*

Whenever I can I travel to. *Asia*

Plane, train, boat, motorcycle, or car? *Boat, car, train.*

My favorite beach. *Pink Sands, in Harbour Island, Bahamas.*

The best snow. *Colorado*

My favorite city. *Istanbul*

The best museum. *National Gallery of Art, Washington, D.C.*

The best hotel or place to stay. *Claridge's in London.*

The world's best shopping street. *Istanbul souk.*

My favorite store. *?*

My favorite market. *All food markets.*

My preferred airline. *Air France.*

My preferred luggage. *The tiniest.*

Jet lag remedy. *Massage—and no e-mail after.*

Always in my suitcase. *Camera and hiking boots.*

Peace, culture, or adventure. *All of it!*

Me on a volcano in Indonesia

Unusual plants in Vietnam

Breathtaking mountaineer's views in New Zealand

Cheryl Finnegan, *VIRGINS, SAINTS, AND ANGELS*

My favorite destination.
Anywhere with my *family,* or *Paris* in the spring— with my dog *Bogue.*

My fondest travel memory.
1. *NYC* with my daughter and getting "*fancy*"
2. Relaxing at the *beach* with my husband and friends

My favorite beach.
Gouverneur Beach, on St. Bart's, or *Isla Mujeres,* Mexico.

The best snow.
Switzerland—at Christmas of course!

The best hotel or place to stay.
Thornbury Castle, UK, or Hotel Sacher, Vienna.

My favorite store.
Colette, Paris, and Neiman Marcus, Dallas (downtown store).

> 66 I'm always searching for the perfect black dress and the perfect swimsuit—the magic one that makes me look like a supermodel. 99

There's no place like home
The PARÓQUIA?

AN INDIAN DANCER

MY DAUGHTER TALLULAH AS AN ANGEL IN A PARADE
our home SAN Miguel de ALLENDE, MX

ANGELS EVERYWHERE

Lots of love in the air

←CRYSTAL

←A CHARM

INSPIRATION
MOSAIC COLOR

Yeohlee Teng, *YEOHLEE*

Whenever I can I travel to. *Key West, Florida*

The best snow. *Outside of my window.*

The best museum. *Pinang Peranakan Mansion, in Penang, Malaysia.*

I'm always searching for the perfect. *State of mind.*

Jet lag remedy. *Follow the clock.*

An ideal trip would be. *Driving from Manhattan, New York, to Tierra del Fuego, Argentina.*

The perfect souvenir. *A memory.*

Always in my carry-on luggage. *ChapStick and dental floss.*

Tiffin carriers on the top, steamboats on the bottom

Sam Shipley & Jeff Halmos, *SHIPLEY & HALMOS*

Whenever we can we travel to. *A BEACH.*

The world's best shopping street.
Wouldn't know—we're not huge shoppers!

Shroud Cay, Bahamas

Peace, culture, or adventure.

Tory Burch

Whenever I can I travel to.

India, for inspiration.

Jodhpur, the Blue City, in India

Marigolds in a market in India

The best snow. *Corriglia in St. Moritz, Switzerland. The views from the gondola ride are breathtaking.*

I'm always searching for the perfect. *Piece of Imari china. My mother and I are both collectors.*

Always in my carry-on luggage. *A picture of my children, my D. Porthault baby pillow, and a red ribbon for good luck.*

Overlooking Machu Picchu

" My fondest
travel memory is
of climbing up to
Machu Picchu,
in Peru, with
my sons. "

My sons and me taking in the view of Machu Picchu

33

Andrew Buckler, *BUCKLER*

My favorite destination. *Montauk, NY*

Plane, train, boat, motorcycle, or car? *A car—easy and close!*

My favorite beach. *Ditch Plains, Montauk*

My favorite city. *LONDON!*

The best museum. *Victoria and Albert, London.*

The best hotel or place to stay. *Çiragǎn Palace, in Kempinski, Istanbul.*

My favorite store. *L'Eclaireur, at 12 Rue Mather, Paris.*

I'm always searching for the perfect. *Legs—antique table legs!*

My favorite market. *Rose Bowl Flea Market, in Pasadena, CA.*

Jet lag remedy. *I always set my clock to the time of my destination—before I fly!*

Beach homes and surfing in Montauk, NY

Carolina Amato

My favorite beach. *In the winter, southwest Florida. In the summer, beaches out in the Hamptons— I love the Atlantic Ocean.*

Always in my suitcase. *I travel only with a CARRY-on. No matter where I am going, I have to be very selective. A great belt is a necessity. It used to be my Hermès—H belt, but I accidentally flushed the "H" down the toilet, and Hermès won't sell the buckle alone. I'm kind of annoyed at them, so I've gone back to my LV belt. I also have special lace pajamas and suede slippers that are just for travel. After a trip, I clean them and put them back in my suitcase.*

Bird life on the southwest coast of Florida

Sang A Im-Propp, *SANG A*

My favorite store. *Neila Vintage and Design on rue du Mont-Thabor, in Paris. I always find the best vintage pieces there—like old Pierre Cardin degrade sunglasses and YSL velvet.*

My preferred airline. *Korean Air, no question. The service, care, and efficiency are unlike any other airline. The stewardesses take such pride in what they do.*

My preferred luggage. *I'm developing my own custom luggage and can't wait to use it. The Large River in zebra alligator is my perfect carry-on—it fits my laptop and all of my travel essentials.*

66 If I ever have time to travel, I always choose home: Seoul. I constantly miss my family, friends, and food. **99**

Me in Seoul, Korea

Elie Tahari

My favorite destination. TEL AVIV

Whenever I can I travel to. ANYWHERE IN EUROPE.

Plane, train, boat, motorcycle, or car? PLANE.

My favorite beach. RANGIROA, TAHITI

Me in Africa

The best snow. ASPEN, CO

My favorite city. NEW YORK

The best museum. MOMA, NY

My favorite guide or travel writing. MY IPAD GUIDES ME

The best hotel or place to stay. AMANDARI RESORT IN BALI.

The world's best shopping street. MONTENAPOLEONE IN MILAN AND BOND STREET IN LONDON.

En route, I wear. I LIKE TO BE COMFORTABLE: JEANS, A SWEATER, AND A JACKET.

The restaurant I would go farthest for. LUCKILY, I DON'T HAVE TO GO FAR: JEAN GEORGES IN NEW YORK.

66 My fondest travel memory is of the first trip I took with my son Jeremy to Jerusalem. I showed him where I grew up. 99

Betsey Johnson

My favorite destination. *NYC uptown*
                              eastside building
Fifth floor = Layla + Ella! My TWO grandkids.
Then — HOT Beaches. SUN!
Then "Marakechup." Anywhere.

Whenever I can I travel to.
  The sun — I feel happy!
  — *Hotel Saint-Barth Isle de France*
  — *St. Maarten's La Samanna Hotel*
  — *Nassau's One&Only Ocean Club*
  — *A quickie: South Beach — Miami's W Hotel*

Plane, train, boat, motorcycle, or car?
Plane, although I HATE to fly.
  I don't like "bumps," so I travel "liquidly."

My favorite store.
  ABC Carpet in NYC, and
    this amazing Italian gourmet store in Milan.

Traveling Tips! B.Y.O.F. < Food. Just in case.
              Red Vines, Parmesan cheese,
                  Yogurt and blueberries, caviar,
                    unsalted roasted almonds, etc.

PACIFIC COAST

W. ← ↑ → E.
       S. ↓

TRONCONES
IXTAPA
ZIHUATANEJO
BARRA DE POTOSI
"BETSEY VILLE"
LA BARITA *"*
VILLA BETSEY *"*

ACAPULCO ↓

BETSEY SHOPS... iN PETULAN!

> 66 My gold heart Betseyville carry-on is my preferred luggage. 99

POCKET

POCKET

Betseyville

ZiP!

ZiP!

THE BEST TRAVEL SMTEELIE - 4 ME

"JUNK" FROM MOROCCO, TURKEY...
BALI... HONG KONG, MEXICO...

-FUL

"Peace, culture, or adventure?

Phillip Lim, *3.1 PHILLIP LIM*

My favorite destination. *Amanyara Resort in Providenciales, Turks and Caicos.*

Plane, train, boat, motorcycle, or car? *Car! I love to drive and listen to good music with good company.*

My favorite guide or travel writing. *Word of mouth, from a trusted source. I also really like the Louis Vuitton City guides for an injection of luxury service.*

The best snow. *It has to be Courchevel, in France, or Whistler Blackcomb, in Canada.*

The restaurant I would go farthest for. *Anywhere my mom is cooking.*

Always in my suitcase. *Apart from the obvious, I always carry a picture of my dog, Oliver.*

Jet lag remedy. *Sleep, water, and Shiseido eye patches one hour before landing.*

A place I will never go. *I never say never!!!*

My dog
Oliver

Off the shores of Long Island

Ulrich Grimm, *CALVIN KLEIN SHOES & ACCESSORIES*

My favorite destination. *Fire Island, New York*

My fondest travel memory. *With my parents and my partner, David, in freezing Den Helder, Netherlands, over Christmas.*

Plane, train, boat, motorcycle, or car? *Boat—preferably from the Venice Airport to the hotel on the Grand Canal.*

The best museum. *Dia Art Foundation's Dia:Beacon, in Beacon, New York.*

The best hotel or place to stay. *GoldenEye, Ian Fleming's original house in Jamaica.*

The perfect souvenir. *Fresh-pressed olive oil from Tuscany, Italy.*

Lana Marks

Me with traditionally dressed Masai Mara warriors in Tanzania, Africa.

On safari in Botswana

Getting my bracelet in Namibia

Inspirational street art in Paris

Tiny restaurant in Tokyo

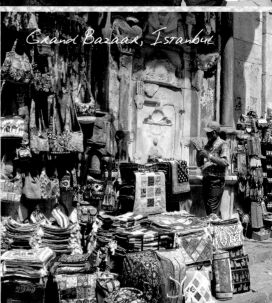

Grand Bazaar, Istanbul

Wildlife in Botswana

Blake Kuwahara, *FOCUS GROUP WEST*

My favorite destination. *Without question—Africa! The terrain, the culture, the souvenirs, the wildlife, and mostly, the people. So far, I've made it to South Africa, Namibia, and Botswana.*

My fondest travel memory. *Getting a bracelet made on me by a Himba tribal woman, with techniques typically used for anklets. Constructed from pounded metal beads and leather, it stayed on my arm for a year.*

The best hotel or place to stay. *Four Seasons Bali, at Jimbaran Bay. Ocean view, outdoor terrace and shower, butler, and private pool. Ah, paradise.*

My favorite guide or travel writing. *I dislike travel guides. Vacations should be spontaneous and not a list of to-dos.*

The world's best shopping street. *Tie: Omotesando Ave., Tokyo, and Klooster Street, Antwerp, Belgium.*

I'm always searching for the perfect. *Vintage ring.*

The restaurant I would go farthest for. *This little noodle shop in a hidden alley in Tokyo.*

Waris Ahluwalia, *HOUSE OF WARIS*

My favorite destination.

It's a toss-up between the Eternal City, Rome, and a quiet white sand beach.

Whenever I can I travel to. *Paris*

My favorite city.

Been here for most of my life and there's no place like it: New York City.

The best museum.

Musée Gustave-Moreau, Paris.

The best snow.

I like palm trees, not snow.

Plane, train, boat, motorcycle, or car?

Sometimes I need all five to get to where I'm going.

Old Delhi Railway Station, Delhi, India

The best hotel or place to stay. *The Taj Lake Palace Hotel in Udaipur, India, is magical, as is the Hotel Gritti Palace, in Venice, Italy.*

The world's best shopping street. *Via Condotti, in Rome.*

My favorite store. *Dover Street Market, in London.*

My favorite market. *Les Puces, Clignancourt, Paris.*

My preferred luggage. *Rimowa.*

Jet lag remedy. *Jet lag is for sissies.*

Peace, culture, or adventure. *For now, adventure.*

The perfect souvenir. *A mug.*

En route, I wear. *A cashmere hoodie.*

Always in my suitcase. *Way too many suits.*

Always in my carry-on luggage. *A bathing suit, a mini backgammon set, and two decks of playing cards.*

Eagle watching in Jaipur, India

On the road, Delhi, India

Jaipur

Trina Turk

Whenever I can I travel to. *Somewhere I haven't been before.*

The perfect souvenir. *Jewelry! It can express the spirit of a place and fit into your carry-on!*

En route, I wear. *Ballet flats, my trusty vintage safari jacket, a cozy tee, and slim pants.*

My preferred luggage. *My Goyard duffle has served me well for so many years—it fits under the seat in front of me on planes, carries loads of magazines, and is virtually indestructible.*

The best snow. *Is viewed from afar.*

Rings in Athens, Greece

Italo Zucchelli, *CALVIN KLEIN COLLECTION (MEN'S)*

My favorite destination. The beach.

My fondest travel memory. The desert in Tunisia.

Whenever I can I travel to. Tulum, Mexico

Plane, train, boat, motorcycle, or car? Travel by foot.

My favorite beach. Liguria, Italy

The best snow. I do not care for it.

My favorite city. New York City

The best museum. Tate Modern, in London.

The best hotel or place to stay. Park Hyatt Tokyo.

The world's best shopping street. Aoyama, Tokyo

My favorite store. Other Music, in New York City.

I'm always searching for the perfect. Place where you don't need a car.

The restaurant I would go farthest for. Posada Margherita, in Tulum, Mexico.

My preferred airline. British Airways.

My preferred luggage. No luggage.

The perfect souvenir. A sunset.

Jet lag remedy. Ginger for two weeks before departure.

Always in my suitcase. An iPod.

R. Scott French

*Our favorite beach on St. Bart's is a thirty-
minute hike down a cliff*

My favorite destination.

*Anywhere in Italy. The air in Italy, both figuratively and
I believe for real, is inebriating. Whenever I'm there, I
feel as if the realities of everyday life in New York are so
distant. Nothing seems to matter but what's for dinner!*

An ideal trip would be. *My next departure.*

A place I will never go. *Mountain climbing.*

It's rare to find the Grand Canal in Venice so calm and serene.

66 My favorite market is Agata & Valentina on First Avenue at East 79th Street in Manhattan. It never disappoints. I love to go in not knowing what I'm in for and find a new treat. Every visit, however, includes a fresh mozzarella, still warm from being made only a few minutes prior to purchase. 99

Adam Lippes, *ADAM*

My favorite beach.
Grande Saline Beach on St. Bart's.

The best museum.
Isabella Stewart Gardner Museum, in Boston, MA.

Always in my suitcase. *Perfect white v—neck tees.*

My fondest travel memory. *My first trip to Europe with my family. I still remember the constant feeling of awe.*

Whenever I can I travel to.
My family in the Berkshires.

My favorite guide or travel writing.
Departures Magazine for amazing hotels. Brazil by John Updike for fiction.

My favorite store. *Bernd Goeckler Antiques on 10th Street in NYC.*

I'm always searching for the perfect.
Object.

Springtime fog in the Berkshires, MA

Shane Baum

The best snow. *St. Anton, Austria*

My favorite city. *Impossible . . . . . .*
- *Fall · Paris*
- *Spring · New York*
- *Summer · Copenhagen*
- *Winter · Palm Springs, CA*

The best museum.
The Louis Vuitton Family Archives, Paris, France (Boy, do I write downhill . . .)

While on a shoe shopping mission in Milan, Italy, I found these men playing classical Italian music, two blocks from The Duomo

My favorite store. *Opening Ceremony in New York City.*

Jet lag remedy. *Two Paths:*
- *Sun · Water · Bikram Yoga · Japanese Fare*
- *Penal · Liquor · Espresso · Loud Music*

En route, I wear.
A Tailored Suit. You know, I'm trying to upgrade the image of us "Sloppy Americans" one flight at a time.

Gilles Mendel, *J. MENDEL*

My fondest travel memory.

A memorable midnight swim with the woman I love, Kylie, on New Year's Eve. It was the middle of a blizzard, and we were staying at the Amangani Hotel in Jackson Hole, Wyoming, surrounded by the Teton Mountains.

Me in Aigua Blava, Spain, 1960. Taken by my mother, Bajla Mendel.

Skiing in Val d'Isère, France, 1970

In Aigua Blava, Spain, with my kids

An ideal trip would be.

A minimum of TWO WEEKS in a country I have yet to discover.
FIRST on the LIST: India.

The restaurant I would go farthest for.

Sushi Kanesaka. For sushi lovers, this restaurant in
Tokyo will be your ultimate experience!

My preferred luggage.

Vintage luggage from T. Anthony.

Plane, train, boat, motorcycle, or car?

For a short road trip, my preference is my 1972
convertible MINI Cooper.

Christina and Swaim Hutson, *HUTSON*

We're always searching for the perfect.

- SNACK
- VINTAGE FIND, CHARM
- TACKY SOUVENIR (we collect SNOWGLOBES)
- DINNER
- DARK SPOT FOR A DRINK
- FUN KIDDIE place —
- SECRET SOCIETY ♡

I ♥ NYC

Our preferred luggage.

NOT WHAT WE HAVE. ☹
we need a SERIOUS up grade.

Jet lag remedy.
coffee to **WINE**

Always in our suitcase.

TOO MUCH TO Remember.
We HAVE KIDS.

with LOVE...
THE HUTSONS.

Narciso Rodriguez

My favorite destination.

Bahia, Brazil

Whenever I can I travel to. *My home in Bahia.*

My favorite beach. *Ipanema in Rio de Janeiro, Brazil.*

The best hotel or place to stay.

Hotel Fasano, in Rio or São Paulo, Brazil.

My favorite store.

Dinosaur Hill in the East Village, New York City.

My backyard in Bahia

"Downtown" Bahia, Brazil

River meets Ocean in Bahia, Brazil

John Patrick, *ORGANIC*

❝ My fondest travel memory is from Florence—of a flawless, surreally dressed man in white. **❞**

Always in my carry-on luggage. *My lucky charms.*

May Van's Camp by Debbie Fleming Caffery

Plane, train, boat, motorcycle, or car? *A bicycle, actually.*

My favorite city. *Rome*

The best museum. *The Clark Art Institute in Williamstown, MA; or for the best selection of Winslow Homers on the planet, The Arkell Museum in Canajoharie, New York.*

I am always searching for the perfect. *Straw hat. I could just travel and buy them, no house needed—just warm places to hang out and wear them.*

My preferred luggage. *Luggage is a tough one. Usually a small bag—carrying unneeded things around the world seems silly to me. I used to travel with my own leather bag that was hand-tooled by a saddle maker in Lima, Peru.*

Marcella Lindeberg, *PARIS 68*

Plane, train, boat, motorcycle, or car?

PLANE!!! AT LEAST EVERY TWO WEEKS. EVEN THOUGH IF
I COULD CHOOSE, I WOULD PICK DRIVING A CAR.
I LOVE DRIVING, MAYBE BECAUSE I AM ITALIAN AND WE
ARE QUITE KNOWN TO BE RATHER WILD DRIVERS.
BUT THE FREEDOM of DRIVING IS UNBEATABLE!

The best hotel or place to stay.

MY FRIEND'S HOUSE IN FORMENTERA... A TRUE RETREAT!
...AND THE COSTES IN PARIS, THE SEXIEST HOTEL
I KNOW —

The perfect souvenir.

SCENTS AND PERFUMES. THAT WILL RECONNECT ME
TO THE PLACES I VISITED.
I AM ALWAYS TRYING TO SCOUT HIDDEN SMALL
LABS WHERE I COULD POSSIBLY FIND A SCENT
I NEVER SMELLED... ☺

66 My favorite destination is
Formentera in Spain's Balearic Islands.
It is the Bohemian alter ego of Ibiza. **99**

Billy Reid

My favorite destination. *New Orleans*

My fondest travel memory. *First trip to London with my wife, Jeanne. Van Morrison and Linda Gail Lewis!*

My favorite beach. *Cape San Blas, Florida*

The best museum. *Museum of Wonder, Seale, Alabama.*

Jet lag remedy. *Bath and beer.*

❝ The best place to stay is a friend's house. ❞

Kyoto, Japan

"During my travels, sometimes I will go to a temple and meditate, even if it's a foreign country. It always relaxes me and rejuvenates my senses."

Mimi So

The restaurant I would go farthest for. *Quanjude Restaurant, the oldest original Peking duck house in Beijing, China.*

An ideal trip would be. *To **not** have any LOST luggage.*

Robert Danes

My fondest travel memory.

— Walking in the **early morning** out to the tip of Point Reyes, in California, and watching the sun burn off the fog to reveal the Pacific a thousand feet below

— Going out in a small dory from Punta Mita, in Mexico, with Rachel and a nine-year-old local driver to fish for tuna in the Pacific

— Rachel and me exploring Tokyo for the first time, searching for the perfect **grilled mackerel** in bars across the city

— The train trip my family took down the length of Mexico in the 1970s

My favorite guide or travel writing. Hemingway, and wherever Rachel says we are going.

John Bartlett

My fondest travel memory. Learning to **body surf** on Martha's Vineyard at age ten, circa 1973. Great fashion year too!

Plane, train, boat, motorcycle, or car?

Love, love, love a train. Very Doctor Zhivago.

Parrot Cay Spa, Turks and Caicos Islands

Ricky Serbin, *RICKY'S EXCEPTIONAL TREASURES*

My favorite destination.

Bruges, Belgium

The best snow.

Melted.

The best hotel or place to stay.

De Witte Lelie, Antwerp, Belgium. So peaceful and charming, with delightful rooms and an amazing breakfast.

Ah, Paris!

Always in my carry-on luggage.

An iPhone; iPad; headphones to drown out cabin noise; a small cashmere blanket and pillowcase; and an eye mask (a sick gift: Mink from Marc Jacobs).

Bruges Markt, a medieval square in the central plaza in Bruges

Lela Rose

My favorite destination. *So far, Vietnam.*

My fondest travel memory. *Riding bikes alongside water buffalos and rice paddies in Vietnam and seeing a family of four with the family pig all riding on one moped—unbelievable!!*

My favorite beach. *Punta de Mita in Mexico— long rolling waves that make surfing seem easy.*

The best museum. *I'm biased!! The Dallas Museum of Art and the Kimbell in Fort Worth, Texas.*

Whenever I can I travel to. *Our family ranch in Texas. I just love going home, and my kids get to feel like true Texans.*

My preferred luggage. *Bric's pink hard-case luggage.*

An ideal trip would be. *Taking my children to Africa. My parents took me when I was thirteen, and it changed my life. I could no longer look at the world through just one lens.*

A place I will never go. *Most likely, the moon.*

Always in my carry-on luggage. *I carry a Nalgene bottle with water. I can't stand buying plastic water bottles.*

Lela Rose and Stitch biking in style in TriBeCa

❝My favorite travel handbooks are the LUXE City Guides.❞

Simon Spurr, *SPURR*

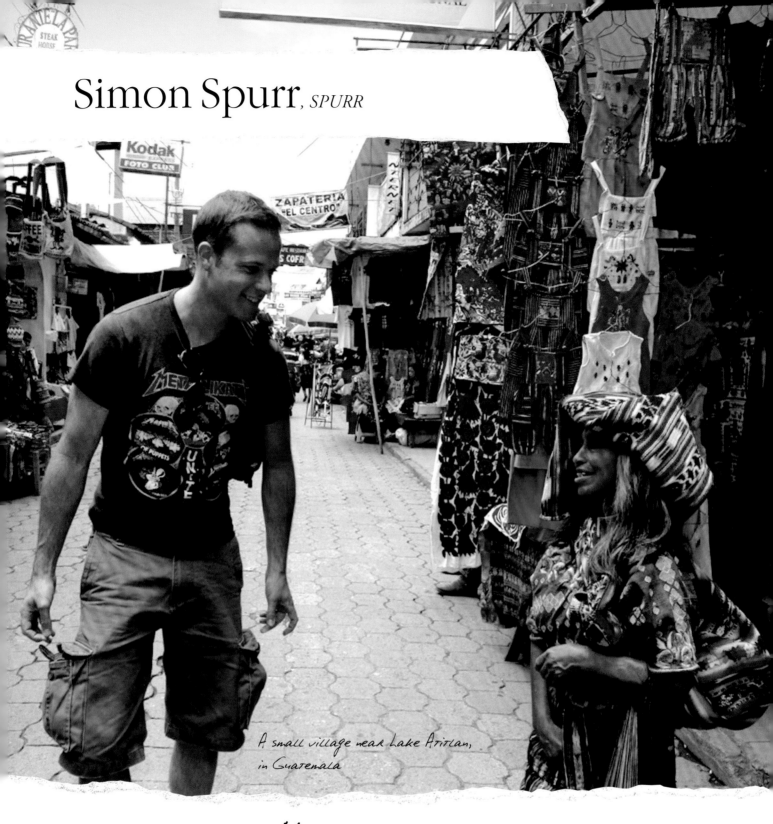

A small village near Lake Atitlan, in Guatemala

Whenever I can I travel to. **Mexico. I love** the country, culture, climate, and people. I'd love to **retire there** one day, or at least build a house there.

The best hotel or place to stay. **The Dylan Hotel in Amsterdam.**

A place I will never go. **Space**—unless they **drop the price!!**

Jackie Rogers

Me and Marcello Mastroani on the set of
Federico Fellini's 8 1/2, filmed on the
beach in Ostia, Italy

A place I will never go. *Mars*

The perfect souvenir. *JADE.*

Always in my suitcase.
A toothbrush.

The best snow. *Cortina
d'Ampezzo, Italy*

My favorite city. *Paris*

Andrew Fezza

My favorite destination. *Saint John, U.S. Virgin Islands*

The best snow. *The snow my **kids** shovel for me.*

My preferred airline. *Alitalia.*

My preferred luggage. *A leather backpack that I bought on the street
in Florence, Italy, about twenty years ago.
It is like a worn-in leather jacket—I won't travel without it!*

View of Trunk Bay, Saint John,
U.S. Virgin Islands

Bamba's Shack, Tortola, British Virgin Islands

Norma Kamali

Porcelain cups made into modern Chinese art are displayed in the lobby of Opposite House Hotel, in Beijing, China

My favorite market. *In 1967, I traveled to Iran during the time of the Shah. I unfortunately was not aware of the fact that I was the only woman in the bazaar, and was swiftly removed. I was overwhelmed by the carpets, textiles, jewelry, and overall design. I can't say I have been back to make it a repeat favorite, but it had the most impact.*

Always in my suitcase. *Olive calcium liniment.*

Amy Chan, *AMY 8 CHAN*

High in the Italian Alps, our friends Madda Gracia and Jorg Badura got married in the snow, complete with a candlelit heart

Sylvia Heisel

Whenever I can I travel to.
A different culture or a remote spot in nature.

The perfect souvenir.
A great memory and some bad photographs.

My favorite destination.
Home, after an amazing adventure someplace else.

The best museum.
The Louvre, in Paris, France.

Black-and-white inspiration in Paris

Naeem Khan

The world's best shopping street. *Chandni Chowk in Delhi, India.*

My favorite market. *Grand Bazaar in Istanbul.*

The best hotel or place to stay. *Umaid Bhawan Palace, in Jodhpur, India.*

Saint Tropez

Lubov Azria, *BCBGMAXAZRIAGROUP*

My favorite city. *Always Tokyo. It's so full of energy and inspiration—I get excited just thinking about going.*

The restaurant I would go farthest for. *Quattro Passi in Marina del Cantone, between Capri and Positano. The chef cooks the whole meal especially for you, and it's like Babette's Feast. It's incredible.*

The perfect souvenir. *I usually take home just a small book or a postcard that inspires me. Sometimes it's just a rock. I have a collection of little water rocks that I've taken from different places I've been. I write the name of the place on the back and keep them in a bag at home.*

Max Azria, *BCBGMAXAZRIAGROUP*

My favorite guide or travel writing. Condé Nast Traveler's
Room with a View or Life as a Visitor,
both published by Assouline.

My favorite beach. St. Bart's or
Fisher Island near Miami.

My favorite store. Barneys New York,
and I like the suits at Paul Smith.

The perfect souvenir. A photograph.

Marine, Anais, Luba, Agnes, Max, and Chloe, in
Punta Cana, Dominican Republic

Keren Craig, *MARCHESA*

My favorite destination. *My beach house in Rhoscolyn, Anglesey, Wales.*

My fondest travel memory. *Backpacking around Thailand with my best friend, Georgina Chapman.*

Whenever I can I travel to. *London, to see my family.*

My favorite beach. *Soneva Gili in the Maldives.*

Jet lag remedy. *Shopping.*

My favorite guide or travel writing. *Bill Bryson.*

The best hotel or place to stay. *Any of the Viceroy Hotels.*

33

RDPIII-043

34

RDPIII-0

Rhoscolyn Beach on the Isle of Anglesey, North Wales, on my wedding day

Sunset from my house in Rhoscolyn Beach

33

36 ▷ 33A

Cliff walking with family in Rhoscolyn Beach

KODAK 320TXP

The church in Rhoscolyn Beach where I got married

Windsurfing in Rhoscolyn Beach is a family tradition

35

RDPIII-043

36

RDPIII-C

Georgina Chapman, *MARCHESA*

My fondest travel memory. *Backpacking around Asia for a year, when I was nineteen.*

Plane, train, boat, motorcycle, or car? *Yacht, for romance.*

My favorite guide or travel writing. *Bill Bryson, for a witty take on travel.*

The best museum. *Victoria and Albert Museum in London, as it inspired me to become a designer.*

The world's best shopping street. *Grand Bazaar in Istanbul.*

Jet lag remedy. *NanoGreens, a green shake that gives you tons of energy.*

Young girls from one of the small mountain villages in the Peruvian Andes

Saint Lucia

Trekking with my mom in the Andes, Peru

The Exumas, in the Bahamas

73

Sophie Buhai, *VENA CAVA*

My fondest travel memory.

OH... SO MANY.
1. EATING DINNER AT A FLOATING PALACE IN UDAIPUR, INDIA, WITH LISA
2. WALKING THROUGH THE SAND DUNES OF DEATH VALLEY IN BLACK TIE
3. SMOKING CIGARS WITH MY DAD IN AN OLD MAFIA HOTEL IN CUBA
4. CAMPING IN BIG SUR
5. EATING BBQ IN MEMPHIS

I'm always searching for the perfect. OLD HOTEL BAR.

The best hotel or place to stay.

HOTEL NACIONAL IN CUBA! BUILT IN 1930 AND WHERE BUSTER KEATON, FRANK SINATRA, MARLENE DIETRICH, AND ERNEST HEMINGWAY USED TO STAY.

The perfect souvenir. ANY KIND OF SPECIAL HOT SAUCE FROM WHERE YOU HAVE BEEN. ALSO- LIP BALM FROM FOREIGN COUNTRIES AND HOTEL STATIONERY.

My preferred luggage. GRANDMA'S OLD GUCCI PASSPORT CASE.

Jet lag remedy. PILATES, BLOODY MARY, LONG WALK.

My favorite city.

LOS ANGELES. I LOVE THE ↗OLD HOLLYWOOD NOSTALGIA, THE HIPPY CULTURE, THE US WEEKLY WANNABES, THE PALM TREES, ART DECO ARCHITECTURE, SUN, HEALTH, MOUNTAINS, CACTI, AND STRIP-MALL FOOD SPOTS.

Lisa Mayock, *VENA CAVA*

My favorite destination. Udaipur, India

The best museum. The doll museum in Paris. Incredibly creepy.

The world's best shopping street. The main highway in Brimfield, MA, with a sea of flea market items on either side, as far as the eye can see. It's heaven.

My favorite store. Maryam Nassir Zadeh - here in NY, on La Manual Alpargatera for espadrilles in Barcelona

I'm always searching for the perfect. matchbooks. I've been collecting them since I was 12.

Always in my carry-on luggage. gum, a notebook, and trashy magazines

The exterior of La Sagrada Família cathedral in Barcelona, Spain

I normally don't take photographs of sunsets, but I couldn't help myself. View from my car on a drive from Palm Springs to Los Angeles.

Robert Rodriguez

My favorite destination. Everything about Italy makes it an ideal travel destination. The history, the culture, the scenery, the people, the food, and clearly the fashion are truly inspiring and so beautiful. There is so much to experience in Italy. You can have the slow-paced rural vacation or experience the fast pace of a city. Every city in Italy is a cultural mecca.

I love it.

Jet lag remedy. The best way I deal with jet lag is to keep my mind off the time difference. If I don't think about what time it is and focus on the present, I tend to adjust more easily.

An ideal trip would be. I'm dying to go to Egypt. The colorful culture is so intriguing, as is the ancient architecture and diversity. When I think of an ideal trip, though, red wine at a cafe in Piazza Navona, in Rome, is pretty hard to top.

Always in my carry-on luggage. In my carry-on you will always find my sketch pad and pencils. They pretty much travel with me everywhere I go. You never know when something will inspire you and an entire look comes to mind. My iPad and eyewear are usually readily available too.

The restaurant I would go farthest for. Cipriani is the best. Whether in New York, Venice, or Hong Kong, I can't seem to stay away from the homemade tagliolini. The restaurant evokes not just cuisine but also a frame of mind.

66 I'm a huge T-shirt fan. If I'm bringing back souvenirs for people, I try to find a T-shirt that represents the spirit of that city. 99

76

Monique Péan

My favorite destination. Tokyo and Kyoto are certainly high on my list! Tokyo looks to the future, while Kyoto embraces the past. Both cities have so many hidden elements to discover and the food is exceptional!

My fondest travel memory. Running through the tunnels in the Egyptian pyramids with my sister Vanessa in Cairo.

Whenever I can I travel to. Paris—the arts, the city, the museums, the crepes! J'adore Paris! I am always inspired by the fashion and the art there.

Me on the beach of Ahe, French Polynesia

Robert Geller

My favorite destination. *Montes Claros. It's in the heart of Brazil, and my wife has a farm there. We ride horses, eat barbecue, and chat with family and friends deep into the night. It's the perfect place to forget about work for a while.*

A beautiful sunset in Montes Claros, Brazil

My friends and me admiring the sky above Montes Claros

City slickers in
Montes Claros

Roadside camels in
Marrakech, Morocco

My Rimowa luggage is always
with me

My wife, Ana, at the Amanjena Hotel,
near Marrakech, Morocco

My fondest travel memory.

Last summer, nine friends and I rented two house-boats and we spent a week traveling down the Canal du Midi in southwestern France. Lots of wine and lots of cheese. Every day was an adventure.

Chris Benz

Me in Florence

Whenever I can I travel to. **PARIS!**

My favorite store. **EBAY!**

I'm always searching for the perfect. **LEATHER JACKET**

Peace, culture, or adventure. **.... PARTY? ¿**

Jet lag remedy. **30 MIN CARDIO + 30 MIN SAUNA**

The perfect souvenir. **FRIENDSHIP BRACELETS**

Monica Rich Kosann

Thailand
by
Monica Rich Kosann

Stephen Dweck

My preferred luggage. *TUMI.*
They made it in a chocolate
brown that they no longer make.
I would travel to just find
and collect more chocolate
brown Tumis!!!

Jet lag remedy. *Shopping—I totally lose*
track of time back home. Day or night,
I can shop. If I do it long enough, maybe
I could propel myself into the next time zone.

En route, I wear.

Navy Prada, head to toe.

Hotel keys—collecting them is like collecting
stamps, which I did as a child

❝ My fondest travel memory is of holding onto my wife Sarise's hand during lift-off and touch down— on every flight. ❞

Form, function, color, mosaic!
Barcelona, Spain

Me in the
Negev
Desert, in
Israel.
It gets hot!

Carole Hochman

Whenever I can I travel to. London, for shopping and great theater! I love the hotels too.

A place I will never go. Again? Venice. I don't like pigeons.

My favorite guide or travel writing. I love to read Travel + Leisure. It enables me to escape to wonderful places, yet never leave my couch.

My favorite city. New York. Even though I've lived here for almost forty years, it constantly feels new. There is never enough time to explore all of its neighborhoods, shops, and restaurants.

The best hotel or place to stay. The Golden Door in Escondido, CA. For one week each year I try to escape to the "Door." It is an oasis of peace, quiet, and fabulous women!

My preferred luggage. T. Anthony. Someday I will buy a complete set in a fabulous color and have them all monogrammed "C.A.S.H."

The Amalfi Coast in Italy

Souvenirs in China

Fabulous colors

The Great Wall of China

Caves (behind doors) in Dunhuang, China

Sailing in Italy

Hiking our way up a hill on the Amalfi Coast

Douglas Hannant

My favorite destination. *My Pennsylvania lake house, on a wildlife preserve in the mountains. It's secluded and stunning in every season.*

The best hotel or place to stay. *I love The Hassler in Rome, Italy. It overlooks the Spanish steps and is so chic.*

I'm always searching for the perfect. *Black turtleneck. I have yet to find it!*

My preferred airline. *Lufthansa first-class.*

A place I will never go. *Siberia*

Always in my suitcase. *Very strange traveling tip: I always carry a roll of tape. I tape the caps of toiletries to prevent them from opening during flight.*

I Palazzi, a fortified tenth century abbey and bishop's palace that belongs to a good friend of mine

Beneath the palace, a half-mile of catacombs

Catherine Malandrino

My fondest travel memory. *My engagement at the Amanpuri, on the beach in Thailand.*

I'm always searching for the perfect. *Morning Light.*

The restaurant I would go farthest for. *Le Chalet de la Plage on the beach at Essaouira, Morocco, for the best whole fish in salt, olive oil, and lemon.*

My preferred luggage. *The Zero Halliburton aluminum suitcase—the James Bond one, lifetime guarantee.*

Always in my carry-on luggage. *My signature "Catherine" sunglasses from Selima, my favorite music, and my iPhone for in-flight pictures of the sky.*

In Moscow, wearing a hat I designed

Me holding starfish in Exuma, in the Bahamas

Breakfast break on safari in the Masai Mara, Kenya

Baby elephants playing at the David Sheldrick Wildlife Trust Orphans Project

Boat people in Hong Kong

Colette Malouf

My favorite destination.
Filled with interesting art and culture, Kenya is a real treat for the creative spirit. I loved the Masai market, filled with diverse artisan crafts from all over the country. Down a dirt road, I discovered the Banana Gallery, a new space with art from some of Kenya's brightest talent. In the Masai Mara, I went to Camp Serian, an eco resort that blends elegantly with its environment.

Plane, train, boat, motorcycle, or car? All of them to get to the most remote locations. It usually goes like this: plane, plane, plane, boat. That's how I got to Lamu in Kenya and Montezuma in Costa Rica.

The best museum. The creamy monochromatic Archaeology Museum in Istanbul, which houses Alexander the Great's sarcophagus, is breathtaking. So much intricately carved stone in pristine condition.

My favorite store. The most beautifully curated lifestyle store is 10 Corso Como in Milan.

My favorite market. The Tsukiji fish market in Tokyo, Japan, is great for sashimi breakfast with a pint of cold beer. It turned me into a sushi snob. But there is more than fish there. I found the coolest accoutrements, like a saltshaker with a rock of pink Himalayan salt.

87

Michel Kramer-Metraux, *MICHEL CRAVAT*

My favorite destination. *A lavender field.*

My favorite city. *Lyon, France*

I'm always searching for the perfect. *Artisan.*

Jet lag remedy. *Mind-set.*

The perfect souvenir. *A hand-carved piece of tree bark.*

Always in my carry-on luggage. *Many ties.*

❝ My fondest travel memory is the smell of Provence, France. ❞

A girl tie

Lavender honey in the making

In love with my muse!

Traditional full-log construction in
Bitterroot Valley, Montana

San Miguel de Allende, Mexico

Henry Jacobson

My favorite destination. *The Bitterroot Valley, Montana. The beautiful, unspoiled vastness of the American West has always held a great attraction for me.*

My favorite store. *Holland & Holland, London. The assortment, attention to detail, and lifestyle statement always inspire me. And the interior seams of its khakis are fully finished!*

Always in my carry-on luggage. *A couple of recent and unread issues of Card Player magazine (I'm a poker player), and something else I've been wanting to read but just haven't found the time. Because the best thing about being on an airplane is time.*

Map, transportation guide,
and fare card from Hong Kong

Isaac Manevitz, *BEN-AMUN BY ISAAC MANEVITZ*

" Despite being a native of Egypt, my wife, Regina, had a typical tourist moment when this camel threw her off and kicked her in the side! Luckily, rides have been calmer since. **"**

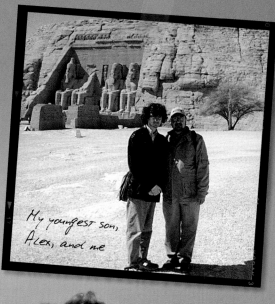

My youngest son, Alex, and me

Francisco Costa, *CALVIN KLEIN COLLECTION (WOMEN'S)*

My favorite destination. Cinelândia, the city center of Rio de Janeiro, Brazil. It's home to several of my favorite galleries, bookshops, and cafes, and has a distinctive Belle Epoque character, with relics in cheerful shades of pink, blue, and yellow. There are great old buildings, completely dilapidated and collapsing, mixed in with a bit of new architecture. It's quite incredible, and very bohemian.

My fondest travel memory. I remember living in Rio and traveling to school from my neighborhood, Botafogo, on the public bus. It's so tight and on Sundays everyone is in a bathing suit. It's quite a ride.

My favorite market. All local farmers' markets are wonderfully colorful and alive.

The perfect souvenir. Havaianas.

Me at Oi Fashion Rocks, in Rio de Janeiro, Brazil

"Garota de Ipanema (The Girl from Ipanema) is the restaurant in Rio where Vinícius de Moraes wrote the famous Bossa Nova song."

91

Pamella Roland

My fondest travel memory.

My family and I were living abroad in Japan, and we took a trip to China, just as tourism was starting to become popular there. Seeing the Chinese people's response to the unfamiliar crowds of visitors was simply unforgettable.

My favorite beach. One of the best-kept secrets is how beautiful the beaches are in northern Michigan. But you can't beat the beautiful water off the coast of Cape Eleuthera, in the Bahamas.

My favorite city. Chicago.
Both of my daughters live there.

The restaurant I would go farthest for. La Société in Paris—the atmosphere, the music, and the food are all exquisite. I love the artsy feel and the nineteenth century vibe—and the fashion crowd it attracts offers great people watching.

Josie Natori, *NATORI*

My favorite guide or travel writing. *Word of mouth.*

My favorite market. *Les Puces, the Paris flea markets.*

My preferred airline. *Cathay Pacific.*

En route, I wear. *Cocoons, cardigans, and scarves. I like to cuddle up when traveling!*

Always in my suitcase. *Everything! I do not travel light.*

The best hotel or place to stay. *Amanresorts.*

My favorite destination. *My home in Paris.*

The best snow. *There's no such thing to me. Too cold!*

" The perfect souvenir is a jewel. "

Angkor Wat, Cambodia

Charming in India

Elephant ride in India

Selima Salaun, *SELIMA OPTIQUE*

My fondest travel memory. *One year during a family vacation, to my surprise, my daughter woke us up at daybreak to help newly born turtles make their way into the ocean.*

The best hotel or place to stay. *Morgan's Rock Hacienda & Ecolodge, an eco-friendly hotel in Nicaragua.*

The restaurant I would go farthest for. *Momofuku in New York City or elBulli in Catalonia, Spain.*

Bali, Indonesia

The perfect getaway in Tunisia, Africa

Bibhu Mohapatra

Whenever I can I travel to. *A different part of India.*

My favorite beach. *Agios Nikolaos, a very secluded beach in Crete. It's sandy and rocky and private.*

Plane, train, boat, motorcycle, or car? *Plane to cross the ocean, trains within.*

My preferred luggage. *Vintage handmade leather cases.*

Always in my suitcase. *My cologne.*

My favorite store. *Browns, London.*

In a time capsule in Venice, Italy

Kay Unger

My preferred airline.

Porter Airlines. Flies from New York to Toronto, and also routes to Detroit and Chicago's Midway. It's elegant and has the best service!

I was in an Israeli army bunker watching an amazing moment: the tanks leaving Gaza en masse, 1994

Plane, train, boat, motorcycle, or car?

I am passionate about traveling by TRAIN.
My dream was to take the Orient Express.

On a teen tour to Europe on the Queen Mary, and home on the Queen Elizabeth—danced every night on the top deck, ca. 1961

PALAIS DE VERSAILLES

❝ The best hotel is Hotel du Cap in Antibes, France. ❞

Vera Wang

My favorite destination.

Paris—because I lived there and owned an apartment in the sixteenth arrondissement for nearly thirty years. I also went to college and skated and worked at American Vogue there as well. Paris is really my second home and will always be a part of my life! Also: Venice—to eat and relax and swim at the Cipriani, and London—to visit friends and shop!

My fondest travel memory.

— Christmases in my father's home in Palm Beach, FL
— Taking my daughters to:
    — Paris, because it is such a big part of my life
    — Shanghai and Beijing, in China, to visit their grandfather
    — the beach at Cala di Volpe in Costa Smeralda, on Sardinia
    — Sandy Lane in Barbados, and realizing they had become young women

My favorite beach. Cala di Volpe, on Sardinia
Venice Beach in Santa Monica
Sandy Lane in Barbados
Las Ventanas in Mexico
The beach in Southampton
The beach in front of my friends' house in Malibu

The world's best shopping street. Avenue Montaigne in Paris, Sloane Street and Bond Street in London, and Aoyama in Tokyo.

Peace, culture, or adventure. All three. Escape.

Edward Wilkerson, *LAFAYETTE 148*

My favorite destination.
Masai Mara, Kenya

My fondest travel memory. *Having lunch in the Mara.*

The world's best shopping street.
Shanghai's stylish Xintiandi district.

I'm always searching for the perfect. *Chair.*

My favorite market.

The flea market in Saint Tropez.

The restaurant I would go farthest for.

New York Grill in the Park Hyatt Tokyo.

En route, I wear. *Layers of cashmere—I'm always cold.*

The best restaurant in the world: Masai Mara, a large game reserve in Kenya

Rafe Totengco, *RAFE NEW YORK & THE JONES GROUP*

My favorite destination.

Asia. There's just so much to discover within the continent. It's rich with inspiration. My list is long, and I'm hoping I can get to every destination in my lifetime.

My fondest travel memory. *A few years ago, my best friend (designer Peter Som) and I traveled to Barcelona for an extended weekend after a trade show in Paris. We had such a blast—eating our way from one tapas bar to another, walking all over the city, meeting up with friends, and seeing the sights. The trip was full of laughter, joy, fond memories, and of course, tons of photos.*

From Left: Ganges River at dawn, Varanasi, India; Taj Mahal, India; Antique snuff bottles at the Panjiayuan Flea Market in Beijing, China; Florence, Italy; Tile wall in the Born district of Barcelona, Spain

If you're thirsty, these Vietnamese boat vendors, in Siem Reap, Cambodia, will sell you anything from bottled water to soda

The city of Patan, in Nepal, rests at the foothills of the Himalayan Mountains. Full of Hindu and Buddhist temples, it is a spiritual oasis of inspiration.

Vanessa Noel

My favorite destination. *India, Nepal, and Round Hill Hotel and Villas Resort, in Jamaica.*

Always in my suitcase. *Airborne and foot cream.*

"There's no place I would never go. "

David Meister

I'm always searching for the perfect.

— Street art and graffiti
— Pair of boots
  (50 pairs and counting!)
— Contemporary work by local and regional artists

" My preferred luggage is my trusty Bottega Veneta medicine bag for carry-on and my simple black Tumi—indestructible! "

Terra-cotta tile roof in Florence, Italy.

Colors, patina, shapes!

Candles in a small church in Munich, Germany.
Love the color and repetition.

Sculpture in a park in Reykjavik, Iceland

Lamps in Istanbul, Turkey

Donna Karan

Whenever I can I travel to. *Bali, Indonesia; Africa; or Parrot Cay, in Turks and Caicos.*

The world's best shopping street. *Bali. I love shopping when I'm there.*

The best snow. *Sun Valley, Idaho*

The best hotel or place to stay. *COMO Shambhala in Bali, Indonesia.*

The perfect souvenir. *A photograph.*

Me in Africa

My favorite guide or travel writing.

Always a friend.

In Kenya, at Shompole Lodge, a true inspiration with its preservation of culture, and its inclusion of the mothers and daughters of the region

In India, with gratitude for what it has meant in my life

Connecting with Africa and nature at my friend's home in Kenya

In Bhutan, with my favorite parts of life: culture and children

Rachel Roy

My fondest travel memory.

My parents traveled with us often—to Africa, England, Scotland, Hawaii, and around the country on road trips. This allowed me early on to view us all as one. When my first daughter was born, it was my goal to fill up her passport as much as possible. It's the only way for her to truly understand the human race, or at least to open up her heart and mind.

Plane, train, boat, motorcycle, or car?

Planes with children, large boats with children and friends, trains when alone, and a motorcycle with my man.

Dennis Basso

Our favorite vacation house, in Saint Tropez, France, which we rent for the month of August

The world's best shopping street. Madison Avenue, New York City.

My favorite beach. Aqua Club, in Saint Tropez, France.

I'm always searching for the perfect. Navy blazer.

Julie Chaiken, *CHAIKEN COTHING*

Taken in Saigon, Vietnam—I love the juxtaposition of the traditional hats and the modern street

The perfect souvenir.

Memories.

In front of my new friend's tailor shop, where they can make anything in three hours

My favorite destination. *I don't have a favorite destination. I prefer to keep moving and exploring. The one place I regularly go back to is Mexico.*

My fondest travel memory. *Scuba diving in Palau. I have never seen anything like the reefs, fish, and water there. It is pristine in every way.*

My favorite beach. *There is a cove just north of Costa Careyes, in Mexico, called Las Rosadas. It's amazing!*

The best snow. *Lake Tahoe. It's right in my backyard in San Francisco, and so beautiful.*

The best museum. *The Musée National Picasso, in Paris, is still my favorite.*

The restaurant I would go farthest for. *Pierre Gagnaire, in Paris.*

My preferred luggage. *Tumi—it lasts forever and is anonymous.*

Marcia Sherrill

Always in my carry-on luggage.

Three books, the novel I am writing, my MacBook, iPad, pink alligator wallet, red alligator bag, orange alligator passport case, Bond No. 9 perfume, deodorant, toothbrush and toothpaste, and cashmere sweaters—I am always cold, cold, cold! Oh, and my travel paints and canvases.

The perfect souvenir. Something from Jermyn Street, in London, like a man's New & Lingwood shirt.

With my daughter Annabelle—the designer of Annabelle by Marcia Sherrill—in my Eric Javits hat at Royal Ascot in England

Me at Royal Ascot

Getting my hands hennaed in Dubai—it's like wearing beautiful jewelry

Erica Courtney

My fondest travel memory.

Travel memories are treasure chests bursting with jewels of happiness! Once when my son was almost six, we were walking along the beach in Florida, and he found a little stick and asked me to stop. He started writing something in the sand—he was having a difficult time, but finally he looked up and smiled. It wasn't spelled exactly right, but it said, "Happy Valentine's Day." It was Valentine's Day, 1984.

Dinnerware collected from around the world

Christian Roth

View of the
Pampelonne Beach in
Saint Tropez

My favorite beach.

Tetiaro Atoll in French Polynesia (Tahiti), it used to be
Marlon Brando's island.
Early morning, I love to take the speedboat from
Papeete, after 1 hour on the high and rough sea,
the amazing sight of Tetiaro. The shade of blues,
the delicate sand barriers, the calm of this destination,
it is just magic and heaven!

A souvenir I could not resist getting
from the Henry Miller Memorial
Library in Big Sur, California

Sandales Tropeziennes by
Rondini, opened in Saint
Tropez in 1927, will make
sandals while you wait

Le Café de
L'Ormeau,
in the medieval
village of
Ramatuelle,
France, hasn't
changed in more
than a
hundred years

Ron Chereskin

Treasury building in Petra, Jordan

Grand Bazaar in Cairo, Egypt

My favorite guide or travel writing.

For restaurant suggestions, Fodor's travel books are great.

66 I'm always searching for the perfect meal. 99

My preferred luggage.

Anything with wheels.

My favorite destination.

Jerusalem

Cynthia Rowley

Me and my daughter Kit in a helicopter

My favorite destination.

Montauk, New York, where every weekend is a forty-eight-hour vacation.

My fondest travel memory.

My husband popping the question at the Taj Mahal, in India.

My favorite guide or travel writing.

Truman Capote's Local Color.

The best snow. *The Himalayas.*

With my husband, Bill, moments after he popped the question at the Taj Mahal

Me on a camel in the middle of the Sahara

The best museum.

The inside of MoMA, in New York, and the outside of the Guggenheim Bilbao, in Spain.

Sully Bonnelly

My favorite destination.

Cuernavaca, in Mexico.
From our home we can see
Popocatépetl Volcano.

My fondest travel memory. Getting my American
citizenship and leaving that very night for Paris.

Plane, train, boat, motorcycle, or car?

Plane, anytime I can help it. Too bad
the Concorde does not exist anymore.
Now I use eBay to add to my original
Concorde memorabilia.

My favorite guide or travel writing.

Lonely Planet and the author
Elizabeth David.

The patio from our suite at the Riad
L'Orangeraie in Marrakech, Morocco,
where the rose petals in the fountain
change color every day

A view of Baja, California, from the window
of a charter flight to Laguna San Ignacio

Mother whale in
Baja, California

This hotel and restaurant in
Cuernavaca, Mexico, is full of
peacocks and delicious Mexican food

Exploring a cave near
Port Lockroy, in
Antarctica

Inspiration for my
Spring 2011 collection

117

Fiona Kotur Marin, *KOTUR*

Plane, train, boat, motorcycle, or car? *I have traveled by train up the Nile; across the Amalfi Coast, in Italy; and through Rajasthan's desert, in India. Our fall 2010 campaign, illustrated by Sheila Camera Kotur, was infused with the nostalgia of rail travel.*

My favorite guide or travel writing. *LUXE City Guides—luxury insider information in pamphlet form, wittily edited by my friend Grant Thatcher.*

My favorite city. *Hong Kong, because of the magnificent view from our apartment there.*

The best museum. *The Metropolitan Museum of Art, in New York—always. And because it's only two blocks from my apartment, I often find myself popping in.*

Fall 2010 KOTUR handbag collection

The perfect powdered snow, in Niseko, Japan

My second son parading around the garden naked with his birthday balloons, in Lakeville, Connecticut

Sue Stemp

I'm always searching for the perfect.

Beach bar that serves local fishy nibbles and cold drinks all day.

My favorite market.

The handicraft market Plaza de San Jacinto, in San Ángel, Mexico City. Embroidery heaven.

The restaurant at the Madonna Inn, in San Luis Obispo, CA

Rainbow over Reykjavik, Iceland

Sweet sixteen in Havana, Cuba

Deborah Lloyd, *KATE SPADE*

Whenever I can I travel to. *My house in upstate New York.*
One day there is a week anywhere else.

Plane, train, boat, motorcycle, or car? *Helicopter!*

My favorite city. *Paris! Oh la la!!*

The best hotel or place to stay. *Raffles Hotel Singapore.*
I love the history and old-world glamour. I've dreamed of staying here since I was a child and I finally visited this year on my way back from Bali. It did not disappoint!

The restaurant I would go farthest for. *La Colombe D'or. Just magical! Perched on the hillside of medieval village Saint-Paul de Vence, in France. Fantastic view, delicious food, and fabulous art.*

> " I even arrived at my wedding on Burgh Island, on the south coast of England, by helicopter. "

Karen Erickson, *ERICKSON BEAMON*

My fondest travel memory. *Friday night Shabbat dinner at the Tower of David, in Jerusalem, Israel.*

Plane, train, boat, motorcycle, or car? *Plane or car. I love taking trips to shop for antiques and vintage finds.*

The best hotel or place to stay. *I love to stay with friends and family. However, my favorite hotels are Two Bunch Palms Resort & Spa, near Palm Springs; the Pavillon de La Reine, in Paris; and the Manilla Hotel, in Jerusalem, Israel.*

The restaurant I would go farthest for. *I love HanGawi Restaurant, in New York City, or any other fabulous vegan or vegetarian restaurant.*

An ideal trip would be. *Anywhere with my family and loved ones.*

Ancient ruins at Masada in Israel

A beautiful sunset over the desert

Questionnaires to do
with friends...

My favorite destination. _____

My fondest travel memory. _____

Plane, train, boat, motorcycle, or car? _____

My favorite guide or travel writing. _____

The best magazine, past or present. _____

My first big trip. _____

My wildest travel disaster. _____

My favorite beach. _____

The best snow. _____

The best place to hike. _____

My favorite city. _____

The best museum. _____

The best hotel or place to stay. _____

My favorite store or market. _____

The perfect souvenir. _____

The restaurant I would go farthest for. _____

My preferred airline. _____

My preferred luggage. _____

Tips on packing. _____

Jet lag remedy. _____

Never leave home without. _____

My happiest travel occupation. _____

My favorite travel companions. _____

My favorite fictional traveler. _____

Peace, culture, or adventure. _____

An ideal trip would be. _____

A place I will never go. _____

Five things I will never forget. _____

My favorite destination. _____

My fondest travel memory. _____

Plane, train, boat, motorcycle, or car? _____

My favorite guide or travel writing. _____

The best magazine, past or present. _____

My first big trip. _____

My wildest travel disaster. _____

My favorite beach. _____

The best snow. _____

The best place to hike. _____

My favorite city. _____

The best museum. _____

The best hotel or place to stay. _____

My favorite store or market. _____

The perfect souvenir. _____

The restaurant I would go farthest for. _____

My preferred airline. _____

My preferred luggage. _____

Tips on packing. _____

Jet lag remedy. _____

Never leave home without. _____

My happiest travel occupation. _____

My favorite travel companions. _____

My favorite fictional traveler. _____

Peace, culture, or adventure. _____

An ideal trip would be. _____

A place I will never go. _____

Five things I will never forget. _____

My favorite destination. _____

My fondest travel memory. _____

Plane, train, boat, motorcycle, or car? _____

My favorite guide or travel writing. _____

The best magazine, past or present. _____

My first big trip. _____

My wildest travel disaster. _____

My favorite beach. _____

The best snow. _____

The best place to hike. _____

My favorite city. _____

The best museum. _____

The best hotel or place to stay. _____

My favorite store or market. _____

The perfect souvenir. _____

The restaurant I would go farthest for. _____

My preferred airline. _____

My preferred luggage. _____

Tips on packing. _____

Jet lag remedy. _____

Never leave home without. _____

My happiest travel occupation. _____

My favorite travel companions. _____

My favorite fictional traveler. _____

Peace, culture, or adventure. _____

An ideal trip would be. _____

A place I will never go. _____

Five things I will never forget. _____

My favorite destination. _____

My fondest travel memory. _____

Plane, train, boat, motorcycle, or car? _____

My favorite guide or travel writing. _____

The best magazine, past or present. _____

My first big trip. _____

My wildest travel disaster. _____

My favorite beach. _____

The best snow. _____

The best place to hike. _____

My favorite city. _____

The best museum. _____

The best hotel or place to stay. _____

My favorite store or market. _____

The perfect souvenir. _____

The restaurant I would go farthest for. _____

My preferred airline. _____

My preferred luggage. _____

Tips on packing. _____

Jet lag remedy. _____

Never leave home without. _____

My happiest travel occupation. _____

My favorite travel companions. _____

My favorite fictional traveler. _____

Peace, culture, or adventure. _____

An ideal trip would be. _____

A place I will never go. _____

Five things I will never forget. _____

My favorite destination. _____

My fondest travel memory. _____

Plane, train, boat, motorcycle, or car? _____

My favorite guide or travel writing. _____

The best magazine, past or present. _____

My first big trip. _____

My wildest travel disaster. _____

My favorite beach. _____

The best snow. _____

The best place to hike. _____

My favorite city. _____

The best museum. _____

The best hotel or place to stay. _____

My favorite store or market. _____

The perfect souvenir. _____

The restaurant I would go farthest for. _____

My preferred airline. _____

My preferred luggage. _____

Tips on packing. _____

Jet lag remedy. _____

Never leave home without. _____

My happiest travel occupation. _____

My favorite travel companions. _____

My favorite fictional traveler. _____

Peace, culture, or adventure. _____

An ideal trip would be. _____

A place I will never go. _____

Five things I will never forget. _____

My favorite destination. _____

My fondest travel memory. _____

Plane, train, boat, motorcycle, or car? _____

My favorite guide or travel writing. _____

The best magazine, past or present. _____

My first big trip. _____

My wildest travel disaster. _____

My favorite beach. _____

The best snow. _____

The best place to hike. _____

My favorite city. _____

The best museum. _____

The best hotel or place to stay. _____

My favorite store or market. _____

The perfect souvenir. _____

The restaurant I would go farthest for. _____

My preferred airline. _____

My preferred luggage. _____

Tips on packing. _____

Jet lag remedy. _____

Never leave home without. _____

My happiest travel occupation. _____

My favorite travel companions. _____

My favorite fictional traveler. _____

Peace, culture, or adventure. _____

An ideal trip would be. _____

A place I will never go. _____

Five things I will never forget. _____

My favorite destination. _____

My fondest travel memory. _____

Plane, train, boat, motorcycle, or car? _____

My favorite guide or travel writing. _____

The best magazine, past or present. _____

My first big trip. _____

My wildest travel disaster. _____

My favorite beach. _____

The best snow. _____

The best place to hike. _____

My favorite city. _____

The best museum. _____

The best hotel or place to stay. _____

My favorite store or market. _____

The perfect souvenir. _____

The restaurant I would go farthest for. _____

My preferred airline. _____

My preferred luggage. _____

Tips on packing. _____

Jet lag remedy. _____

Never leave home without. _____

My happiest travel occupation. _____

My favorite travel companions. _____

My favorite fictional traveler. _____

Peace, culture, or adventure. _____

An ideal trip would be. _____

A place I will never go. _____

Five things I will never forget. _____

My favorite destination. _____

My fondest travel memory. _____

Plane, train, boat, motorcycle, or car? _____

My favorite guide or travel writing. _____

The best magazine, past or present. _____

My first big trip. _____

My wildest travel disaster. _____

My favorite beach. _____

The best snow. _____

The best place to hike. _____

My favorite city. _____

The best museum. _____

The best hotel or place to stay. _____

My favorite store or market. _____

The perfect souvenir. _____

The restaurant I would go farthest for. _____

My preferred airline. _____

My preferred luggage. _____

Tips on packing. _____

Jet lag remedy. _____

Never leave home without. _____

My happiest travel occupation. _____

My favorite travel companions. _____

My favorite fictional traveler. _____

Peace, culture, or adventure. _____

An ideal trip would be. _____

A place I will never go. _____

Five things I will never forget. _____

My favorite destination. _____

My fondest travel memory. _____

Plane, train, boat, motorcycle, or car? _____

My favorite guide or travel writing. _____

The best magazine, past or present. _____

My first big trip. _____

My wildest travel disaster. _____

My favorite beach. _____

The best snow. _____

The best place to hike. _____

My favorite city. _____

The best museum. _____

The best hotel or place to stay. _____

My favorite store or market. _____

The perfect souvenir. _____

The restaurant I would go farthest for. _____

My preferred airline. _____

My preferred luggage. _____

Tips on packing. _____

Jet lag remedy. _____

Never leave home without. _____

My happiest travel occupation. _____

My favorite travel companions. _____

My favorite fictional traveler. _____

Peace, culture, or adventure. _____

An ideal trip would be. _____

A place I will never go. _____

Five things I will never forget. _____

My favorite destination. _____

My fondest travel memory. _____

Plane, train, boat, motorcycle, or car? _____

My favorite guide or travel writing. _____

The best magazine, past or present. _____

My first big trip. _____

My wildest travel disaster. _____

My favorite beach. _____

The best snow. _____

The best place to hike. _____

My favorite city. _____

The best museum. _____

The best hotel or place to stay. _____

My favorite store or market. _____

The perfect souvenir. _____

The restaurant I would go farthest for. _____

My preferred airline. _____

My preferred luggage. _____

Tips on packing. _____

Jet lag remedy. _____

Never leave home without. _____

My happiest travel occupation. _____

My favorite travel companions. _____

My favorite fictional traveler. _____

Peace, culture, or adventure. _____

An ideal trip would be. _____

A place I will never go. _____

Five things I will never forget. _____

My favorite destination. _____

My fondest travel memory. _____

Plane, train, boat, motorcycle, or car? _____

My favorite guide or travel writing. _____

The best magazine, past or present. _____

My first big trip. _____

My wildest travel disaster. _____

My favorite beach. _____

The best snow. _____

The best place to hike. _____

My favorite city. _____

The best museum. _____

The best hotel or place to stay. _____

My favorite store or market. _____

The perfect souvenir. _____

The restaurant I would go farthest for. _____

My preferred airline. _____

My preferred luggage. _____

Tips on packing. _____

Jet lag remedy. _____

Never leave home without. _____

My happiest travel occupation. _____

My favorite travel companions. _____

My favorite fictional traveler. _____

Peace, culture, or adventure. _____

An ideal trip would be. _____

A place I will never go. _____

Five things I will never forget. _____

My favorite destination. _____

My fondest travel memory. _____

Plane, train, boat, motorcycle, or car? _____

My favorite guide or travel writing. _____

The best magazine, past or present. _____

My first big trip. _____

My wildest travel disaster. _____

My favorite beach. _____

The best snow. _____

The best place to hike. _____

My favorite city. _____

The best museum. _____

The best hotel or place to stay. _____

My favorite store or market. _____

The perfect souvenir. _____

The restaurant I would go farthest for. _____

My preferred airline. _____

My preferred luggage. _____

Tips on packing. _____

Jet lag remedy. _____

Never leave home without. _____

My happiest travel occupation. _____

My favorite travel companions. _____

My favorite fictional traveler. _____

Peace, culture, or adventure. _____

An ideal trip would be. _____

A place I will never go. _____

Five things I will never forget. _____

My favorite destination. _____

My fondest travel memory. _____

Plane, train, boat, motorcycle, or car? _____

My favorite guide or travel writing. _____

The best magazine, past or present. _____

My first big trip. _____

My wildest travel disaster. _____

My favorite beach. _____

The best snow. _____

The best place to hike. _____

My favorite city. _____

The best museum. _____

The best hotel or place to stay. _____

My favorite store or market. _____

The perfect souvenir. _____

The restaurant I would go farthest for. _____

My preferred airline. _____

My preferred luggage. _____

Tips on packing. _____

Jet lag remedy. _____

Never leave home without. _____

My happiest travel occupation. _____

My favorite travel companions. _____

My favorite fictional traveler. _____

Peace, culture, or adventure. _____

An ideal trip would be. _____

A place I will never go. _____

Five things I will never forget. _____

My favorite destination. _____

My fondest travel memory. _____

Plane, train, boat, motorcycle, or car? _____

My favorite guide or travel writing. _____

The best magazine, past or present. _____

My first big trip. _____

My wildest travel disaster. _____

My favorite beach. _____

The best snow. _____

The best place to hike. _____

My favorite city. _____

The best museum. _____

The best hotel or place to stay. _____

My favorite store or market. _____

The perfect souvenir. _____

The restaurant I would go farthest for. _____

My preferred airline. _____

My preferred luggage. _____

Tips on packing. _____

Jet lag remedy. _____

Never leave home without. _____

My happiest travel occupation. _____

My favorite travel companions. _____

My favorite fictional traveler. _____

Peace, culture, or adventure. _____

An ideal trip would be. _____

A place I will never go. _____

Five things I will never forget. _____

Fashionable Address Book

MUSEUMS

ASIA

THE KYOTO COSTUME INSTITUTE
Kyoto, Japan
www.kci.or.jp

LEEUM SAMSUNG MUSEUM OF ART
Seoul, South Korea
leeum.samsungfoundation.org

PINANG PERANAKAN MANSION
Penang, Malaysia
www.pinangperanakanmansion.com.my

EUROPE

GUGGENHEIM MUSEUM BILBAO
Bilbao, Spain
guggenheim.org/bilbao

HAMBURGER BAHNHOF
Berlin, Germany
www.hamburgerbahnhof.de

ISTANBUL ARCHAEOLOGY MUSEUM
Istanbul, Turkey
sacred-destinations.com/turkey/
istanbul-archaeological-museum.htm

MUSÉE GUIMET
Paris, France
www.guimet.fr/-English

MUSÉE GUSTAVE-MOREAU
Paris, France
www.musee-moreau.fr

MUSÉE DU LOUVRE
Paris, France
louvre.fr

MUSÉE MAEGHT
Saint-Paul, France
maeght.com

MUSÉE NATIONAL PICASSO
Paris, France
musee-picasso.fr

MUSÉE DE L'ORANGERIE
Paris, France
www.musee-orangerie.fr

MUSÉE D'ORSAY
Paris, France
musee-orsay.fr

MUSÉE DE LA POUPÉE
Paris, France
museedelapoupeeparis.com

MUSEO DI CAPODIMONTE
Naples, Italy
en.museo-capodimonte.it

MUSEO NACIONAL DEL PRADO
Madrid, Spain
museodelprado.es

NEUES MUSEUM
Berlin, Germany
neues-museum.de

THE PITTI PALACE
Florence, Italy
www.uffizi.firenze.it

PUNTA DELLA DOGANA
Venice, Italy
www.palazzograssi.it/en

THE UFFIZI GALLERY
Florence, Italy
uffizi.com

THE VASA MUSEUM
Stockholm, Sweden
vasamuseet.se/en

THE VILLA PANZA
Varese, Italy

MIDDLE EAST

THE EGYPTIAN MUSEUM
Cairo, Egypt
touregypt.net/egyptmuseum/egyptian_
museum.htm

THE MUSEUM FOR ISLAMIC ART
Jerusalem, Israel
islamicart.co.il/en

SOUTH AMERICA

THE CARMEN MIRANDA MUSEUM
Rio de Janeiro, Brazil

UNITED KINGDOM

NATURAL HISTORY MUSEUM
London, England
nhm.ac.uk

SIR JOHN SOANE'S MUSEUM
London, England
soane.org

THE TATE MODERN
London, England
tate.org.uk/modern

VICTORIA AND ALBERT MUSEUM
London, England
www.vam.ac.uk

UNITED STATES

THE ART INSTITUTE OF CHICAGO
Chicago, Illinois
artic.edu/aic

DE YOUNG MUSEUM
San Francisco, California
deyoung.famsf.org

DIA:BEACON
Beacon, New York
diabeacon.org/sites/main/beacon

EXPLORATORIUM: THE MUSEUM OF SCIENCE, ART AND HUMAN PERCEPTION
San Francisco, California
exploratorium.edu

GRAND RAPIDS ART MUSEUM
Grand Rapids, Michigan
artmuseumgr.org

ISABELLA STEWART GARDNER MUSEUM
Boston, Massachusetts
gardnermuseum.org

THE J. PAUL GETTY MUSEUM
Los Angeles, California
getty.edu/museum

THE METROPOLITAN MUSEUM OF ART
New York, New York
metmuseum.org

THE MUSEUM OF CONTEMPORARY ART
Los Angeles, California
moca.org

THE MUSEUM OF MODERN ART
New York, New York
moma.org

THE MUSEUM OF WONDER
Seale, Alabama
museumofwonder.com

NATIONAL GALLERY OF ART
Washington D.C.
nga.gov

THE NEW YORK BOTANICAL GARDEN
Bronx, New York
nybg.org

PALACE OF FINE ARTS THEATRE
San Francisco, California
palaceoffinearts.org

SMITHSONIAN
Washington D.C.
si.edu/museums

HOTELS

AFRICA

RIAD EL FENN
Marrakech, Morocco
riadelfenn.com

RIAD L'ORANGERAIE
Marrakech, Morocco
riadorangeraie.com

SINGITA BOULDERS LODGE
Sabi Sand Game Reserve, Kruger National Park, South Africa
singita.com

ASIA

AMANDARI RESORT
Bali, Indonesia
www.amanresorts.com/amandari/home.aspx

CHEONG FATT TZE MANSION
Penang, Malaysia
cheongfatttzemansion.com

COMO SHAMBHALA ESTATE
Bali, Indonesia
cse.como.bz

CONRAD TOKYO
Tokyo, Japan
conradhotels1hilton.com/en/ch/hotels/
index.do?ctyhocn=TYOCICI&WT.srch=1

FOUR SEASONS RESORT BALI AT JIMBARAN BAY
Bali, Indonesia
fourseasons.com/jimbaranbay

GORA KADAN
Fuji-Hakone National Park, Japan
gorakadan.com/introduction

THE OBEROI
Bali, Indonesia
oberoihotels.com/oberoi_bali

PENINSULA HONG KONG
Hong Kong, China
peninsula.com

RAFFLES HOTEL SINGAPORE
Singapore
raffles.com/EN_RA/Property/RHS

THE RITZ-CARLTON, SEOUL
Seoul, South Korea
ritzcarlton.com/en/Properties/Seoul

SONEVA GILI
Lankanfushi Island, North Malé Atoll, Republic of Maldives
sixsenses.com/Soneva-Gili

W HONG KONG
Hong Kong, China
starwoodhotels.com/whotels/property/
overview/index.html?propertyID=1965

CARIBBEAN

EDEN ROCK
St. Bart's
edenrockhotel.com

HOTEL TAIWANA
St. Bart's
hoteltaiwana.com

ROUND HILL HOTEL AND VILLAS
Montego Bay, Jamaica
roundhilljamaica.com

CENTRAL AMERICA

MORGAN'S ROCK
Republic of Nicaragua
morgansrock.com

EUROPE

3 ROOMS HOTEL
Milan, Italy
10corsocomo.com/#3rooms

AGRESTO GUEST HOUSE, BROLIO CASTLE
Siena, Italy
ricasoli.it/proposte/a-weekend-in-brolio

L'AUBERGE DU PÈRE BISE
Talloires, France
perebise.com/uk

BELVEDERE HOTEL
Mykonos, Greece
belvederehotel.com

ÇIRAĞAN PALACE KEMPINSKI
Istanbul, Turkey
kempinski.com/en/istanbul

LA COLOMBE D'OR
Saint-Paul, France
la-colombe-dor.com

THE DYLAN HOTEL
Amsterdam, Netherlands
www.dylanamsterdam.com

FOUR SEASONS HOTEL GEORGE V
Paris, France
fourseasons.com/paris

FOUR SEASONS HOTEL MILANO
Milan, Italy
fourseasons.com/milan

GRAND-HÔTEL DU CAP-FERRAT
Saint-Jean-Cap-Ferrat, France
grand-hotel-cap-ferrat.com/uk

GRAND HOTEL QUISISANA
Capri, Italy
quisisana.com

GRAND YAZICI HOTEL
Bodrum, Turkey
grandyazici.com/bodrum

HASSLER ROMA
Rome, Italy
hotelhasslerroma.com

HÔTEL BEAU RIVAGE
Geneva, Switzerland
beau-rivage.ch/uk

HOTEL COSTES
Paris, France
hotelcostes.com

HÔTEL DE CRILLON PARIS
Paris, France
crillon.com

HÔTEL DE PARIS
Monte Carlo, Monaco
en.hoteldeparismontecarlo.com

HOTEL DE WITTE LELIE
Antwerp, Belgium
dewittelelie.be

HÔTEL DU CAP-EDEN-ROC
Antibes, France
hotel-du-cap-eden-roc.com/uk

HÔTEL DU PALAIS
Biarritz, France
hotel-du-palais.com

HOTEL EDEN ROC POSITANO
Positano, Italy
edenrocpositano.com

HOTEL GRITTI PALACE
Venice, Italy
hotelgrittipalacevenice.com

HOTEL PAVILLON DE LA REINE
Paris, France
pavillon-de-la-reine.com

HÔTEL PLAZA ATHÉNÉE
Paris, France
plaza-athenee-paris.com

HOTEL PRINCIPE DI SAVOIA MILANO
Milan, Italy
hotelprincipedisavoia.com

HOTEL SACHER VIENNA
Vienna, Austria
sacher.com/en-hotel-sacher-vienna.htm

HOTEL SAVOY
Florence, Italy
hotelsavoy.it

J.K. PLACE CAPRI
Capri, Italy
jkcapri.com

LUX YOGA
Tourrettes-sur-Loup, France
lux-yoga.com

LE MEURICE
Paris, France
lemeurice.com

PARK HYATT PARIS
Paris, France
paris.vendome.hyatt.com

PIKES HOTEL
Ibiza, Spain
luxehotels.com/hotels/Pikes

LA RÉSERVE RAMATUELLE
Ramatuelle, France
lareserve-ramatuelle.com/en/home

RITZ PARIS
Paris, France
ritzparis.com

LE SIRENUSE
Positano, Italy
sirenuse.it

VILLA D'ESTE
Cernobbio, Italy
villadeste.com

INDIA

THE LEELA PALACE KEMPINSKI BANGALORE
Bangalore, India
theleela.com/hotel-bangalore.html

TAJ LAKE PALACE
Udaipur, India
tajhotels.com/palace/Taj%20Lake%20Palace,Udaipur

THE TAJ MAHAL PALACE
Mumbai, India
tajhotels.com/Palace/The%20Taj%20Mahal%20Palace,MUMBAI

UMAID BHAWAN PALACE
Jodhpur, India
tajhotels.com/Palace/Umaid%20Bhawan%20Palace,Jodhpur

MEXICO

CABANAS LA CONCHITA
Tulum, Mexico

CONDESA DF
Mexico City, Mexico
condesadf.com

LAS MAÑANITAS
Cuernavaca, Morelos, Mexico
lasmananitas.com.mx

MIDDLE EAST

ADRÈRE AMELLAL
Cairo, Egypt
adrereamellal.net

MAMILLA HOTEL
Jerusalem, Israel
mamillahotel.com

SOUTH AMERICA

HOTEL FASANO
Rio de Janeiro, Brazil
São Paulo, Brazil
fasano.com.br

SOUTH PACIFIC

THE WAKAYA CLUB & SPA
Fiji Islands
wakaya.com

UNITED KINGDOM

CLARIDGE'S
London, England
www.claridges.co.uk

CLIVEDEN
Taplow Berkshire, England
www.clivedenhouse.co.uk

HOTEL MISSONI
Edinburgh, Scotland
hotelmissoni.com

SOHO HOUSE
London, England
sohohouse.com

THORNBURY CASTLE
Thornbury, Gloucestershire, England
thornburycastle.co.uk

UNITED STATES

CHATEAU MARMONT
Hollywood, California
chateaumarmont.com

GOLDEN DOOR
Escondido, California
goldendoor.com/escondido

THE MADONNA INN
San Luis Obispo, California
madonnainn.com

THE STANDARD SPA MIAMI BEACH
Miami Beach, Florida
standardhotels.com/miami

ST. REGIS NEW YORK
New York, New York
stregisnewyork.com

TWO BUNCH PALMS
Desert Hot Springs, California
twobunchpalms.com

VANESSA NOEL HOTEL
Nantucket, Massachusetts
vanessanoelhotel.com

SHOPPING STREETS

ASIA

AOYAMA
Tokyo, Japan

CANTON ROAD
Hong Kong, China

GINZA
Tokyo, Japan

OMOTESANDŌ
Tokyo, Japan

TAKESHITA-DŌRI
Tokyo, Japan

XINTIANDI
Shanghai, China

EUROPE

LE MARAIS
Paris, France

THE NINE STREETS
Amsterdam, Netherlands

RUE DE LILLE
Paris, France

RUE DE L'UNIVERSITÉ
Paris, France

RUE DE SAINTONGE
Paris, France

RUE DU BAC
Paris, France

RUE DU FAUBOURG SAINT-
HONORÉ
Paris, France

RUE VIEILLE DU TEMPLE
Paris, France

VIA CONDOTTI
Rome, Italy

VIA MONTENAPOLEONE
Milan, Italy

UNITED KINGDOM

BOND STREET
London, England

FLORAL STREET
London, England

JERMYN STREET
London, England

SLOANE STREET
London, England

ST. ANDREW'S SQUARE
Edinburgh, Scotland

WEST PORT
Edinburgh, Scotland

UNITED STATES

ABBOT KINNEY BOULEVARD
Venice, California

DIXIE HIGHWAY
West Palm Beach, Florida

MADISON AVENUE
New York, New York

MAIDEN LANE
San Francisco, California

RODEO DRIVE
Beverly Hills, California

SILVERADO TRAIL
Napa Valley, California

STORES

ASIA

COMME DES GARÇONS
Tokyo, Japan

GOODS OF DESIRE
Hong Kong, China
god.com.hk

JOYCE
Hong Kong, China
joyce.com

NISHIJIN-ORI-KAIKAN
Kyoto, Japan

LANE CRAWFORD
China
lanecrawford.com

LOVELESS
Tokyo, Japan
loveless-shop.jp

TOKYU HANDS
Tokyo, Japan
www.tokyu-hands.co.jp/en

EUROPE

10 CORSO COMO
Milan, Italy
10corsocomo.com

LE BON MARCHÉ
Paris, France
lebonmarche.com

CHANEL
Paris, France
chanel.com

COLETTE
Paris, France
colette.fr

DEYROLLE
Paris, France
deyrolle.com

FAUCHON
Paris, France
fauchon.com

GALERIE OLIVIA LAMY CHABOLLE
Paris, France
galerielamychabolle.com

HERMÈS
Paris, France
hermes.com

HIDETAKA FUKAYA, COBBLER
Florence, Italy

LA MANUAL ALPARGATERA
Barcelona, Spain
homepage.mac.com/manualp

MERCI
Paris, France
merci-merci.com

MURIEL GRATEAU
Paris, France
murielgrateau.com

NEILA VINTAGE AND DESIGN
Paris, France

OFFICINA PROFUMO-
FARMACEUTICA DI SANTA MARIA
NOVELLA
Florence, Italy
www.smnovella.it

THE OLD AND THE BEAUTIFUL
Antwerp, Belgium

SAN CARLO DAL 1973
Turin, Italy
sancarlo1973.it

INDIA

HOT PINK
Jaipur, India
hotpinkindia.com

UNITED KINGDOM

BROWNS
London, England
brownsfashion.com

HERMAN BROWN
Edinburgh, Scotland
hermanbrown.co.uk

HOLLAND & HOLLAND
London, England
hollandandholland.com

JAMES SMITH & SONS
UMBRELLAS
London, England
james-smith.co.uk

JOSEPH
Fulham Road, London, England
joseph.co.uk

UNITED STATES

THE ANTIQUES GARAGE
New York, New York
hellskitchenfleamarket.com/home

BARNEYS NEW YORK
New York, New York
barneys.com

BON VIVANT
Palm Springs, California
gmcb.com/shop

THE CARVERSVILLE GENERAL
STORE
Carversville, Pennsylvania
carversville.com/general

DE VERA
New York, New York
deveraobjects.com

DINOSAUR HILL
New York, New York
dinosaurhill.com

GAGOSIAN SHOP
New York, New York
gagosian.com/shop

IKRAM
Chicago, Illinois
ikram.com

MARYAM NASSIR ZADEH
New York, New York
maryamnassirzadeh.com

MAXFIELD
Los Angeles, California
maxfieldla.com

NEIMAN MARCUS
Dallas, Texas
neimanmarcus.com

OAK: MANHATTAN
New York, New York
oaknyc.com

ODIN NEW YORK
New York, New York
odinnewyork.com

OLD TOWNE WINE AND SPIRITS
Louisville, Kentucky
oldtownwine.com

OPENING CEREMONY
Los Angeles, California
New York, New York
openingceremony.us

PRINTED MATTER
New York, New York
printedmatter.org

PRIVET HOUSE
Warren, Connecticut
privethouse.com

SEVEN SEAS GALLERY
Nantucket, Massachusetts

MARKETS

AFRICA

MARRAKECH SOUKS
Marrakech, Morocco

THE MEDINA
Marrakech, Morocco

ASIA

CHATUCHAK WEEKEND MARKET
Bangkok, Thailand

DONG-DAE-MUN MARKET
Seoul, Korea
donami.or.kr/Eng

FLOWER MARKET
Mong Kok, Hong Kong, China

PATPONG NIGHT MARKET
Bangkok, Thailand

SOUTH BUND FABRIC MARKET
Shanghai, China

TSUKIJI FISH MARKET
Tokyo, Japan
www.tsukiji-market.or.jp/tukiji_e.htm

EUROPE

LAS DALIAS
San Carlos, Ibiza, Spain
lasdalias.squarespace.com

FISH MARKET
Saint Tropez, France

THE GRAND BAZAAR
Istanbul, Turkey
grandbazaaristanbul.org

LE JAS DES ROBERTS
Saint Tropez, France
jasdesroberts.com

MERCAT DE LA BOQUERIA
Barcelona, Spain
boqueria.info

OPEN MARKET
Gordes, France

PESCHERIA RIALTO FISH MARKET
Venice, Italy

LES PUCES DE PARIS, SAINT-OUEN
Paris, France
parispuces.com

SPICE BAZAAR
Istanbul, Turkey

INDIA

AJUNA FLEA MARKET
Goa, India

CHANDNI CHOWK MARKET
Delhi, India

CHAURA RASTA
Jaipur, India

JOHARI BAZAAR
Jaipur, India

MEXICO

HANDICRAFT MARKET PLAZA DE SAN JACINTO
San Ángel, Mexico City

MERCADO DE LA LAGUNILLA
Mexico City, Mexico

UNITED KINGDOM

CAMDEN MARKETS
London, England
camdenmarkets.org

DOVER STREET MARKET
London, England
doverstreetmarket.com

PORTOBELLO ROAD
London, England
portobelloroad.co.uk

UNITED STATES

AGATA & VALENTINA
New York, New York
agatavalentina.com

THE CAPITAL CITY FARMERS MARKET
Montpelier, Vermont
montpelierfarmersmarket.com

MELROSE PLACE FARMERS' MARKET
Los Angeles, California

ROSE BOWL FLEA MARKET
Pasadena, California

SAG HARBOR FARMERS' MARKET
Sag Harbor, New York

STOCKTON CERTIFIED FARMERS' MARKET
Stockton, California
stocktonfarmersmarket.org

UNION SQUARE GREENMARKET
New York, New York
grownyc.org/unionsquaregreenmarket

WEST 25TH STREET MARKET
New York, New York
hellskitchenfleamarket.com

RESTAURANTS

AFRICA

LE CHALET DE LA PLAGE
Essaouira, Morocco

ASIA

KIKUNOI HONTEN
Kyoto, Japan

QUANJUDE RESTAURANT
Beijing, China
quanjude.com.cn

RED CAPITAL CLUB
Beijing, China
redcapitalclub.com.cn

SUSHI KANESAKA
Tokyo, Japan

AUSTRALIA

BONDI ICEBERGS BISTRO
Bondi Beach, Australia
icebergs.com.au/food-drink

CARIBBEAN

BABANUCO
Cabrera, Dominican Republic

EUROPE

DA ADOLFO
Positano, Italy
daadolfo.com

EL BULLI
Roses, Spain
elbulli.com

CHEZ L'AMI LOUIS
Paris, France

ENOTECA PINCHIORRI
Florence, Italy
enotecapinchiorri.com

GIACOMO RISTORANTE
Milan, Italy
giacomomilano.com

HAMDI RESTAURANT
Istanbul, Turkey
hamdi.com.tr

HARRY'S BAR
Venice, Italy
harrysbarvenezia.com

HOSTERIA DEL PESCE
Rome, Italy
hosteriadelpesce.net

LA MÈRE BRAZIER
Lyon, France
lamerebrazier.fr

LA MÈRE MICHAUD
Aix-les-Bains, France
lameremichaud.com

LA PETITE MAISON
Nice, France
lapetitemaison-nice.com

PIERRE GAGNAIRE
Paris, France
pierregagnaire.com

QUATTRO PASSI
Marina del Cantone, Italy
ristorantequattropassi.com/en

RESTURANTE LA PALOMA
Ibiza, Spain
palomaibiza.com

RISTORANTE PANE E VINO ENOTECA
Florence, Italy
ristorantepaneevino.it

RISTORANTE ZAIRA
Siena, Tuscany, Italy

LA SOCIÉTÉ
Paris, France
restaurantlasociete.com

STEIRERECK
Vienna, Austria
steirereck.at

TAPIOLES 53
Barcelona, Spain
tapioles53.com

LE VOLTAIRE
Paris, France

INDIA

BUKHARA
New Delhi, India
itcwelcomgroup.in/welcomcuisine/bukhara/cuisine_origin_brief.html

SPICE MARKET RESTAURANT
New Delhi, India

MEXICO

POSADA MARGHERITA
Tulum, Mexico
posadamargherita.com

MIDDLE EAST

RESTAURANT MOUNIR
Broummana, Lebanon
mounirs.com

SOUTH AMERICA

SIRI MOLE & CIA
Rio de Janeiro, Brazil
sirimole.com.br

UNITED KINGDOM

NOBU
London, England
noburestaurants.com/london

THE WITCHERY BY THE CASTLE
Edinburgh, Scotland
thewitchery.com

UNITED STATES

BAR MASA
New York, New York
masanyc.com

CIPRIANI
Los Angeles, California
New York, New York
cipriani.com

CUT
Beverly Hills, Los Angeles, California
wolfgangpuck.com/restaurants/fine-dining/3789

DOE'S EAT PLACE
Greenville, Mississippi
doeseatplace.com

GALATOIRE'S RESTAURANT
New Orleans, Louisiana
galatoires.com

HANGAWI RESTAURANT
New York, New York
hangawirestaurant.com

JEAN GEORGES
New York, New York
jean-georges.com

JOE'S STONE CRAB
Miami Beach, Florida
joesstonecrab.com

MADEO
Los Angeles, California

MR. CHOW
Los Angeles, California
mrchow.com

R & G LOUNGE
San Francisco, California
rnglounge.com

THE SLANTED DOOR
San Francisco, California
slanteddoor.com

LE VEAU D'OR
New York, New York

CFDA Members

1	Amsale Aberra	56	Georgina Chapman	110	Isaac Franco	163	Michel Kramer-Metraux
2	Reem Acra	57	Ron Chereskin	111	R. Scott French	164	Regina Kravitz
3	Adolfo	58	Wenlan Chia			165	Devi Kroell
4	Waris Ahluwalia	59	Susie Cho	112	Mr. James Galanos	166	Nikki Kule
5	Steven Alan	60	David Chu	113	Nancy Geist	167	Christopher Kunz
6	Simon Alcantara	61	Eva Chun	114	Robert Geller	168	Nicholas Kunz
7	Linda Allard	62	Doo-Ri Chung	115	Geri Gerard	169	Blake Kuwahara
8	Carolina Amato	63	Peter Cohen	116	Justin Giunta		
9	Ron Anderson	64	Kenneth Cole	117	Gary Graham	170	Steven Lagos
10	John Anthony	65	Liz Collins	118	Nicholas Graham	171	Derek Lam
11	Nak Armstrong	66	Michael Colovos	119	Henry Grethel	172	Richard Lambertson
12	Brian Atwood	67	Nicole Colovos	120	Ulrich Grimm	173	Adrienne Landau
13	Lisa Axelson	68	Sean Combs			174	Liz Lange
14	Lubov Azria	69	Rachel Comey	121	Jeff Halmos	175	Ralph Lauren
15	Max Azria	70	Anna Corinna Sellinger	123	Tim Hamilton	176	Eunice Lee
16	Yigal Azrouël	71	Maria Cornejo	124	Douglas Hannant	177	Judith Leiber
		72	Esteban Cortazar	125	Cathy Hardwick	178	Larry Leight
17	Mark Badgley	73	Francisco Costa	126	Karen Harman	179	Nanette Lepore
18	Michael Ball	74	Victor Costa	127	Dean Harris	180	Michael Leva
19	Jeffrey Banks	75	Jeffrey Costello	128	Johnson Hartig	181	Monique Lhuillier
20	Leigh Bantivoglio	76	Erica Courtney	129	Sylvia Heisel	182	Phillip Lim
21	Jhane Barnes	77	James Coviello	130	Joan Helpern	183	Johan Lindeberg
22	John Bartlett	78	Steven Cox	131	Stan Herman	184	Marcella Lindeberg
23	Victoria Bartlett	79	Keren Craig	132	Lazaro Hernandez	185	Adam Lippes
24	Dennis Basso	80	Philip Crangi	133	Carolina Herrera	186	Deborah Lloyd
25	Michael Bastian			134	Tommy Hilfiger	187	Elizabeth Locke
26	Shane Baum	81	Sandy Dalal	135	Carole Hochman	188	Tina Lutz
27	Bradley Bayou	82	Robert Danes	136	Christina Hutson	189	Jenna Lyons
28	Vicki Beamon	83	David Dartnell	137	Swaim Hutson		
29	Richard Bengtsson	84	Oscar de la Renta			190	Bob Mackie
30	Dianne Benson	85	Donald Deal	138	Sang A Im-Propp	191	Jeff Mahshie
31	Chris Benz	86	Louis Dell'Olio	139	Alejandro Ingelmo	192	Catherine Malandrino
32	Alexis Bittar	87	Pamela Dennis			193	Maurice Malone
33	Kenneth Bonavitacola	88	Lyn Devon	140	Marc Jacobs	194	Colette Malouf
34	Sully Bonnelly	89	Kathryn Dianos	141	Henry Jacobson	195	Isaac Manevitz
35	Monica Botkier	90	Keanan Duffty	142	Eric Javits, Jr.	196	Robert Marc
36	Marc Bouwer	91	Randolph Duke	143	Lisa Jenks	197	Mary Jane Marcasiano
37	Bryan Bradley	92	Stephen Dweck	144	Betsey Johnson	198	Lana Marks
38	Barry Bricken			145	Alexander Julian	199	Deborah Marquit
39	Thom Browne	93	Marc Ecko			200	Lisa Mayock
40	Dana Buchman	94	Libby Edelman	146	Gemma Kahng	201	Jessica McClintock
41	Andrew Buckler	95	Sam Edelman	147	Norma Kamali	202	Jack McCollough
42	Sophie Buhai	96	Mark Eisen	148	Donna Karan	203	Mary McFadden
43	Tory Burch	97	Melinda Eng	149	Kasper	204	Kimberly McDonald
44	Stephen Burrows	98	Karen Erickson	150	Ken Kaufman	205	Mark McNairy
		99	George Esquivel	151	Jenni Kayne	206	David Meister
45	Anthony Camargo			152	Anthony Keegan	207	Andreas Melbostad
46	Kevin Carrigan	100	Steve Fabrikant	153	Rod Keenan	208	Gilles Mendel
47	Pierre Carrilero	101	Carlos Falchi	154	Pat Kerr	209	Gene Meyer
48	Liliana Casabal	102	Pina Ferlisi	155	Naeem Khan	210	Carlos Miele
49	Edmundo Castillo	103	Erin Fetherston	156	Eugenia Kim	211	Stefan Miljanich
50	Salvatore Cesarani	104	Andrew Fezza	157	Adam Kimmel	212	Nicole Miller
51	Richard Chai	105	Cheryl Finnegan	158	Calvin Klein	213	Malia Mills
52	Julie Chaiken	106	Eileen Fisher	159	Michael Kors	214	Rebecca Minkoff
53	Amy Chan	107	Dana Foley	160	Monica Rich Kosann	215	James Mischka
54	Charles Chang-Lima	108	Tom Ford	161	Fiona Kotur-Marin	216	Richard Mishaan
55	Natalie Chanin	109	Istvan Francer	162	Reed Krakoff	217	Isaac Mizrahi

218	Bibhu Mohapatra	257	Laura Poretzky	296	George Sharp	336	Sophie Theallet
219	Paul Morelli	258	Zac Posen	297	Marcia Sherrill	337	Gordon Thompson III
220	Robert Lee Morris	259	Lilly Pulitzer	298	Sam Shipley	338	Monika Tilley
221	Miranda Morrison	260	James Purcell	299	Kari Sigerson	339	Zang Toi
222	Rebecca Moses	261	Jessie Randall	300	Daniel Silver	340	Isabel Toledo
223	Kate Mulleavy			301	Howard Silver	341	Rafe Totengco
224	Laura Mulleavy	262	David Rees	302	Michael Simon	342	John Truex
225	Sandra Muller	263	Tracy Reese	303	George Simonton	343	Trina Turk
226	Matt Murphy	264	William Reid	304	Paul Sinclaire	344	Mish Tworkowski
		265	Robin Renzi	305	Pamela Skaist-Levy		
227	Gela Nash-Taylor	266	Mary Ann Restivo	306	Michael Smaldone	345	Patricia Underwood
228	Josie Natori	267	Brian Reyes	307	Amy Smilovic	346	Kay Unger
229	Charlotte Neuville	268	Judith Ripka	308	Michelle Smith		
230	Irene Neuwirth	269	Patrick Robinson	309	Maria Snyder	347	Carmen Marc Valvo
231	David Neville	270	Loree Rodkin	310	Mimi So	348	Nicholas Varney
232	Rozae Nichols	271	David Rodriguez	311	Peter Som	349	John Varvatos
233	Lars Nilsson	272	Narciso Rodriguez	312	Kate Spade	350	Joan Vass
234	Roland Nivelais	273	Robert Rodriguez	313	Gunnar Spaulding	351	Adrienne Vittadini
235	Vanessa Noel	274	Jackie Rogers	314	Peter Speliopoulos	352	Diane von Furstenberg
236	Charles Nolan	275	Pamella Roland	315	Michael Spirito	353	Patricia von Musulin
237	Maggie Norris	276	Lela Rose	316	Simon Spurr		
238	Juan Carlos Obando	277	Kara Ross	317	Laurie Stark	354	Marcus Wainwright
239	Ashley Olsen	278	Christian Roth	318	Richard Stark	355	Tom Walko
240	Mary-Kate Olsen	279	Cynthia Rowley	319	Cynthia Steffe	356	Alexander Wang
241	Sigrid Olsen	280	Rachel Roy	320	Shelly Steffee	357	Vera Wang
242	Luca Orlandi	281	Ralph Rucci	321	Sue Stemp	358	Cathy Waterman
243	Rick Owens	282	Kelly Ryan	322	Scott Sternberg	359	Heidi Weisel
				323	Robert Stock	360	Stuart Weitzman
244	Thakoon Panichgul	283	Gloria Sachs	324	Steven Stolman	361	Carla Westcott
245	Marcia Patmos	284	Jamie Sadock	325	Jay Strongwater	362	John Whitledge
246	John Patrick	285	Selima Salaun	326	Jill Stuart	363	Edward Wilkerson
247	Edward Pavlick	286	Angel Sanchez	327	Anna Sui	364	Gary Wolkowitz
248	Monique Péan	287	Behnaz Sarafpour	328	Koi Suwannagate	365	Jason Wu
249	James Perse	288	Janis Savitt	329	Daiki Suzuki		
250	Robin Piccone	289	Arnold Scaasi	330	Albertus Swanepoel	366	Araks Yeramyan
251	Mary Ping	290	Jordan Schlanger			367	Gerard Yosca
252	Maria Pinto	291	Lorraine Schwartz	331	Elie Tahari	368	David Yurman
253	Jill Platner	292	L'Wren Scott	332	Robert Tagliapietra		
254	Linda Platt	293	Ricky Serbin	333	Vivienne Tam	369	Gabriella Zanzani
255	Tom Platt	294	Christopher Serluco	334	Rebecca Taylor	370	Katrin Zimmermann
256	Alexandre Plokhov	295	Ronaldus Shamask	335	Yeohlee Teng	371	Italo Zucchelli

The Council of Fashion Designers of America, Inc. (CFDA) is a not-for-profit trade association whose membership consists of over 370 of America's foremost fashion and accessory designers. CFDA Foundation, Inc. is a separate, not-for-profit company, which was organized to raise funds for charity and industry activities. Founded in 1962, the CFDA's goals are "to further the position of fashion design as a recognized branch of American art and culture, to advance its artistic and professional standards, to establish and maintain a code of ethics and practices of mutual benefit in professional, public, and trade relations, and to promote and improve public understanding and appreciation of the fashion arts through leadership in quality and taste."

Acknowledgments

My partner, Jay, and me in Key West, FL, the southernmost point in the USA, and only ninety miles from Cuba

American Fashion Travel: Designers on the Go is an invitation to take a fashionable trip around the world. I am so appreciative that our members are sharing their favorite destinations and travel tips and have agreed to open up their personal photo albums and scrapbooks. This book is a rare opportunity to glimpse into the trips and vacations of over 100 CFDA members. It is part of the successful American Fashion series the Council of Fashion Designers of America publishes with Assouline. Our past books include *American Fashion*, *American Fashion Accessories*, *American Fashion Menswear*, *Geoffrey Beene: An American Fashion Rebel*, *American Fashion Cookbook*, and *American Fashion Home*.

As always, we are so grateful for all of the guidance and support we receive from Assouline. Special thanks to Prosper and Martine Assouline for their partnership, and much gratitude to our editorial director Esther Kremer, our editor Ariella Gogol, our designers Camille Dubois and Jihyun Kim, our director of production Gina Amorelli, and our photo editor Rebecca Stepler, for all their hard work. A big thank you also goes to Lisa Marsh. The book would not have been possible without the organization and huge efforts of CFDA's Sophie Marx, with guidance from Christine Olsen, and with the support of the entire CFDA staff—Lisa Smilor, CaSandra Diggs, Catherine Bennett, Karen Peterson, Amy Ondocin, Heather Jacobson, Sara Maniatty, and Johanna Stout. Thank you also to our invaluable interns Cachée Livingston, Emily Chi, Lauren Levy, and Erin Kent. And thank you to CFDA President Diane von Furstenberg. She is truly a "woman on the go" who is never far from her work in leading the CFDA.

Bon Voyage!

Steven Kolb

CFDA Executive Director